LEADERSHIP TOOL KIT

Andrew

With friendship, warmth
& respect

Bryn   9/9/09

Leadership
Tool Kit

BRYN HUGHES

KINGSWAY PUBLICATIONS
EASTBOURNE

First published by Monarch Books 1998
This edition by Kingsway 2002

ISBN 1 84291 051 5

Published by
KINGSWAY COMMUNICATIONS LTD
Lottbridge Drove, Eastbourne, BN23 6NT, England.
Email: books@kingsway.co.uk

Book design and production for the publishers by
Bookprint Creative Services,
P.O. Box 827, BN21 3YJ, England.
Printed in Great Britain.

DEDICATION

To my wife, Vicky,
without whom the path would not be remotely the
same. She has accompanied me in countless journeys
during our marriage, and helped substantially at every
stage of this book.

CONTENTS

FOREWORD

It is very rare to come across a book that provides the reader with both an experience of personal development and at the same time a number of very practical tools for the development of others. *Leadership Tool Kit* does just that. It equips the leader to enable others while leaving the leader more mature and secure in his or her calling.

Leadership is there for others: it is not an end in itself. Yet so much written on leadership in recent years has neglected membership. *Leadership Tool Kit* will, I hope, be the first of a new generation of texts to restore the balance and place the focus of leadership on both self and others.

For the experienced leader, *Leadership Tool Kit* will come as a breath of fresh air, cutting away the theories and philosophies and exposing quickly the heart of the matter – since we are made in the image of God, we need look no further than his Word for the principles and practices upon which to build our own development and the development of those we seek to lead.

For those new to leadership, or aspiring to leadership roles, *Leadership Tool Kit* will introduce you to many practical and wise approaches to people development, which, if built into your own style, will save you the pain of many hard lessons.

Bryn Hughes has brought together in this book a wealth of personal experience gained over many years of leadership training in many countries and cultures. I have been privileged to share in some of these learning adventures and I am delighted that the text not only gives the reader access to his distilled knowledge, but also introduces us to the writer himself – his values, his motives and his example.

I commend this book to all those in leadership roles – in whatever environment they operate.

David Cormack

ACKNOWLEDGEMENTS

To David Cormack, who together with his wife, Edith, have given of their lives, knowledge and materials throughout many years. Our debt to them is great.

To Jane Collins, together with the Monarch team who published the original edition. Without her encouragement and skill, this book would not have happened.

To Nigel Ring and Tim Goss for their contributions and criticisms. Their friendship means even more.

The content of this book is equally applicable to male and female. For the sake of convenience only, the author has used 'he' rather than the more cumbersome 'he/she'.

INTRODUCTION

The urge to write this book has been with me for some time. In some ways I hoped that it would go away, but the desire has grown stronger in the light of the needs I have found as I work with leaders, especially in the Church. I have been involved in education for most of my working life and in leadership and management training during the last two decades. Now by choice I spend approximately eighty per cent of my time in churches, missionary societies, relief agencies and residential care, generally the non-profit-making sector with a Christian ethos; the remainder is in the so-called secular world.

Church and mission leaders often say things like this to me:

'All that management stuff is fine in the secular setting but we don't need it in the Church.'

'Money isn't the bottom line around here you know. We're in the people business.'

'We share God's love.'

'Obviously Christian leadership is totally different.'

I only wish that all of these statements were true. Certainly money is not the bottom line in Church life, and some of the rest of society is slowly finding the same truth. Leaving God out of it just for the moment, the real bottom line is our neighbour, whether that is the customer or simply someone whose needs we can meet. In that respect, the Church and the rest of society have some similarities. Customers remove their commitment from poor products, and congregations leave poor quality churches and organisations. It is the past, present or prospective member that decides what 'good' or 'poor' means, not the minister of the church, or the leadership team of the organisation.

In all cases, both Christian and secular, the issues of improvement revolve around leadership.

The excitement for me in my work and ministry is finding that the roots of good, apparently secular, leadership tools are biblical. Good management and leadership are about the short and long-term care of people more than projects or things, so it really shouldn't be surprising that God had the first and last words to say on such issues. The core principles of people management will not change with time.

Leadership in the Church should be demonstrably better than 'outside'. If this was already the case, then probably our evangelistic problems would be over. The quality of life in the Church would be such an advertisement that folk would flock to join. Success, however you measure it, and the capability of leadership are closely linked. I fully understand that there is a limit to the human contribution in building the Church or any Christian organisation. We do not carry the final 'can'. We can preach the gospel: we cannot guarantee that the outcomes will be what we want. However, I am a great believer in personal and corporate responsibility. We have been chosen as God's instruments and he desires to work through us. Too often, 'Christian' work practices have been synonymous with second rate. Muddling through is deemed acceptable. I have been thrilled recently to find mis-

sions and churches where excellence is not only being talked
about, but is beginning to emerge in visible, practical ways.
Yet it is still not the norm, despite the roots of true excellence
being very biblical.

I am not trying to minimise the problems of Church
leaders. Selection mechanisms are based on very loose criteria. I have asked many ministers who have sat on selection
panels about the personal specifications that they are trying
to measure. Usually, but not always, they can tell me what
they do on an assessment course, but seldom why they
undertook that activity. Further probing still fails to identify
any criteria. Some use mediocre psychometric tests but
cannot tell me how the results are integrated into the decision of selection. The main thrust of many of the replies is
that they are trying to find caring people. Some have con-
fided that the decisions have often been based on a narrow
majority. Others have said that eventually the votes represent
empathy with similar churchmanship. Liberals look for
liberals, evangelicals want more evangelicals, etc: they
recruit in their own image.

Generally, the colleges which train Church and mission
leaders do not prepare them for what they are about to face.
Training in the people skills that they will need is often brief
and very basic. Few of the Christian training institutions in
Europe spend the equivalent of a week, within a three-year
course, studying management. And by management I mean
people skills. Too few of the lecturers retain sufficient
contact with the real world of leadership. For many years,
the attitudes to finance in Christian colleges have been unrealistic. I am not suggesting that we should adopt secular,
materialistic standards, but the lack of finance means the
support staff that would be deemed necessary in other
institutions have not been provided for the training of ministers. Similarly, the provision of secretarial and administrative help for functioning leaders has frequently been

inadequate. Where in industry would we fail to provide a personal assistant to a managing director of a company with, say, 300 staff?

Admittedly, the parallels are not completely justified. The bulk of the 'staff' in Church life are not full time and there are no contracts for them. But pursuit of the path which ignores the similarities leads to a big fallacy. We need to recognise and accept that there are many lessons to be learnt from the practices and experience of industry and commerce. The main similarity is the importance of leadership.

The things that keep people in churches are complex, but without doubt, the quality of leadership is the single biggest feature.

The calibre of leadership required when dealing with part-time volunteers is much higher than in a typical company situation. In the Church context, you cannot just call a meeting of senior staff at the drop of a hat. The communication problems are much worse in voluntary organisations.

The thrust of this book is that the quality of leadership in the Church must be enhanced to meet the challenges that we are facing today, and will increasingly face. It will involve changes, but change is on God's agenda. Again, I've found Christians are often among the most reluctant groups to embrace change. In the last twelve months I've listened to three radio programmes with a Christian ethos about change; they have all focused on the nature of the unchanging God. But everything else changes. I'm glad that he hasn't finished with me yet! He allows the world to change and he asks us to remain relevant to the world. Change, however, can be very threatening, especially in traditional institutions.

Difficulties are not solved by sweeping them under the carpet and hoping that they will go away. Sweeping issues into hiding is acceptable only if you are going to tackle them at a more convenient time. More commonly the outcome is an increased paralysis. The longer an issue is left, the worse it becomes and the harder it is to raise our game and finally solve the problem. It is time to face real issues. The statistics of Church attendance are quite clear about the decline, virtually right across the institution within the continent of Europe. It seems to me that in all other institutions, when an organisation is doing badly, we analyse the leadership. We should do the same with churches, and in the widest sense of leadership. At least privatised utilities have made us focus on the leaders!

I intimated that my interest is in the widest concept of leadership. Churches, like armies, have a structure that should be strongly dependent on the second echelon of leadership. Armies are not composed just of generals and privates. Equally, churches depend on the wider concept of leadership.

The size and competence of the second tier determines the width and quality of programme that can be offered.

I have never been in a church where this second tier of leadership is too wide or too competent. People join churches with an established, broad leadership, and the second tier stays both busy and fulfilled. Just to clarify, I believe in leaders, I believe in leadership, I believe in teams and I believe in leaders who are accountable in teams. This book is not designed to enhance the position of autocratic dictators; they told me not to bother! There is a need to enhance the skills and understanding of people in the very senior positions, number ones in their organisations. Equally, we must focus on the second and third tiers, the wider concept of leadership. Even language like 'number one' and 'tier' can be dangerous. Chapter 1 will explain the nature of leadership more fully. It is significant that in the Bible, according to my computerised concordance, there are 79 references for 'leader' but 120 references when used in the plural. There are 6 quotes mentioning a single 'elder' and 188 when used in the plural.

The importance of the second tier of leadership

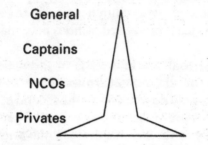

Figure 1. A shortage in the middle ranks

Too frequently, I find the emphasis in churches and other organisations to be modelled on Figure 1. One general, lots of privates and nothing much in between!

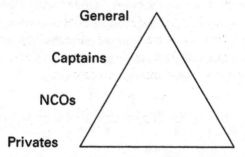

Figure 2. Balanced numbers throughout the structure

This would be more typical of a services' model, and much better balanced. A few captains, rather more lower-ranked officers and altogether sufficient officers to lead the foot soldiers.

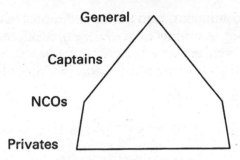

Figure 3. Too many leaders!

I long to see churches like the final diagram! There is more than sufficient middle-ranking leadership already in place to be able to cope with a rapid and dramatic expansion. I suspect that God has delayed revival until we implement this lesson. He does not want the parable of the sower repeated on a grand scale. His desire is that all who own his name continue to walk fruitfully with him.

Every 'line manager' is responsible for developing the people under them, whether in a business or church setting. This is not an optional extra within the job description. The development of the second tier of leadership is a non-negotiable aspect of the leader's job. Not that they have to do it all, but they must ensure that it is done. Chapter 2 will lay out the conditions and climate that leadership has to produce in an organisation to facilitate this.

We are looking for a mentality of ongoing staff development.

This is not the same as having a high training priority or budget (which few churches have anyway!). Sending people on courses, or even putting on in-house training is not the same as providing a mentality of personal development. It needs to be continuous, high profile and rooted in the workplace. Training is a subset of staff development, but it is less than the full picture.

Organisations benefit

This is not only true in the secular situation: churches and missions are just the same. One leader said, 'I would rather set ten people to work than do the work of ten people.' This sounds nice and also very obvious, but some leaders would actually rather do it all themselves. 'Empowerment' is on many lips but not in quite so many hearts, and in even fewer actions. The real bonus comes if the ten people we develop catch the same empowerment vision, and we all resist the temptation to do the work of a hundred people. When the second generation get involved the dividends are really exponential. If we reach this stage, progress in the effectiveness of the organisation can be dramatic.

Leaders last longer

The price of overworking is not paid instantaneously. We can all raise our game for a short season, and on occasions should do so. But there must be light at the end of the tunnel, not just a theoretical knowledge that there jolly well ought to be light there! (One minister told me that for him, the light at the end of the tunnel usually turned out to be a train coming the other way!) So perhaps if a major project or pressing need means we will have to work longer hours for a few months, that's not a problem. When the additional hours become routine and an accepted way of life, then we are in trouble. The second-mile mentality should be voluntary and not demanded.

    In 1991, a Bible college conducted a survey of pastors. The findings included:

90% of pastors worked more than 46 hours per week.

33% say that being in the ministry is an outright hazard to family life.

75% have experienced at least one stress-related crisis in their ministry.

90% believe they were inadequately trained for ministry demands.

70% now have a lower self-esteem than when they started their ministry.

40% report a serious conflict with a church member at least once a month

70% do not have anyone that they consider a close friend.

Wouldn't we all like to see less of these stress-related symptoms?

People stay committed

The Bible gives us the analogy of the body. Can one limb or member manage without the others? No. Yet the message given in many churches is that a few people have a monopoly on the gifts and basically the remainder, often about eighty per cent of the total membership, are spectators. If they come and watch, well that's great, but in terms of productivity it doesn't really matter whether they attend or not – provided that their giving is by standing order of course! Remarkably also, once an individual is branded as in the eighty per cent, it is quite difficult to get a transfer to the involved, trusted twenty per cent. One of the biggest lessons from the new churches is that participation brings commitment.

Always remember that there is a price of changing and a price of *not* changing. Often we jib at paying the price of change because the bill comes immediately and it is paid as a lump sum. The cost of not changing is commonly paid by instalments, but is always more expensive in the long run. Change processes, including the application to individual lives, often go through three phases as shown below.

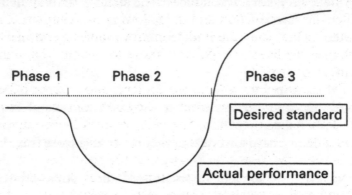

Figure 4. The phases of change

Phase 1. Things are not all they could be, but we are bumbling along.
Phase 2. Changes are made. Performance, satisfaction and many other measurable criteria go down as we begin to handle unfamiliar situations. E.g., when we initially delegate a task, often the new person will not immediately do it so well. It is usually because of this potential fall in standard that we choose not to change. Often, too, the instigator is the only beneficiary, and this leaves them having to process the guilt feelings.
Phase 3. Everybody benefits.

Let me now give you an overview of the layout and strategy of this book. After this introduction, there are two chapters which set out the foundations. Chapter 1 clarifies what we mean by leadership as opposed to managers, administrators and pastors. We won't be able to enhance leaders if we don't know what they do and what they look like! Then chapter 2 will look at the corporate culture, the feel and ethos of any church or organisation. How do we analyse this and how do we make sure that it is conducive to leadership development? After this introduction and the following two chapters, I'm assuming that you want both to improve yourself and also to enhance the lives and skills of those for whom you share some responsibility.

I've packaged the bulk of the contents into sections called tools, not chapters. The meat of the book consists of tools for developing leadership. The better leaders I come across have a deep concern for developing others and are crying out for tools – the 'how to'. Throughout the book, each of the tools has two stages of application, first for you, and at a second level, as you help other leaders to grow. I suggest that you can use this book as a manual. Why not make it into your one-year coaching course? Tackle the first tool by reading the relevant section and spend a month deliberately sharpening your skills in this feature. During the second month, read the next section and add another improved tool to your repertoire, without slackening the application of the first. By the end of the year you will have a range of tools available to you, and also some idea of which are most comfortable and effective for you. In each section, I have covered the theoretical aspects soundly but simply, trying to give you sufficient background, but moving quickly to application, the skill dimension. At the end of some sections, I've given a few useful book titles if you want to read further around the subject.

More effective leadership starts here.

CHAPTER 1

WHAT IS A LEADER?

We need to spend a little time thinking about leadership, largely to distinguish it from management. While there is some overlap, the distinctive elements of leadership are most frequently the missing ingredients. There are many theories about what makes a leader. Here are some commonly held views that offer a contribution to our understanding of leadership, none of which contains the whole truth by any means.

Leaders are recognisable at a glance

Should we be able to go into a room and pick out the leaders? The tallest, the intellectuals, the communicators, etc.? Saul might be an example – 'an impressive young man without equal among the Israelites – a head taller than any of the others' (1 Samuel 9:2).

Leaders are made by the situation

Cometh the hour, cometh the man. There were examples during the Second World War. After bombers crash landed, often it was not the pilot who attempted to lead the survivors back to friendly territory, but another member of the crew.

There was frequently a ready acceptance of that situational leadership, including by the pilot.

Leaders are born not made

John the Baptist was selected for greatness even before he was born. 'You are to give him the name John. He will be a joy and delight to you, and many will rejoice because of his birth, for he will be great in the sight of the Lord . . . he will be filled with the Holy Spirit even from birth' (Luke 1:13–17).

Leadership is a gift

This theory is that you cannot make leaders; you are either given the gift of leadership or you are not. There is no production line; the making of leaders is outside our control. People who were anointed in the Old Testament would be examples, although many of them would also fit other theories as well. Romans 12:8 refers specifically to the gift of leadership, but I feel that the focus of my book is directed to the many people in leadership positions who, like Gideon, Isaiah and Peter, do not feel that they are specifically gifted.

Leadership is a package of skills

This theory, more in vogue at the present, says that the behaviours and attitudes of leadership can be learned. Selection procedures for many jobs now tend to identify the competencies required, so presumably we can identify the competencies of leadership and train people in these skills.

I have found people subscribing to a measure of all these approaches in Church life, but probably some are more

popular. Not all would formulate their theories as starkly as
the above sketches, but the practical outworking of their
leadership is the real testimony of what they believe. There
would be a strong lobby in some churches for the anointing
concept, the person who is 'set apart' from the mass. The
implication would be that you are chosen for leadership and
that leaders cannot be made from a mould.

It is more constructive to think about two other features of
leadership – the character and the functions of leaders. Who
you are and what you do are more important than what you
say. In the New Testament the requirements for holding
office are those of personal life-style, not the possibilities we
listed above. Leaders 'must be above reproach, the husband
of but one wife, temperate, self-controlled, respectable,
hospitable, able to teach, not given to drunkenness, not
violent but gentle, not quarrelsome, not a lover of money' (1
Timothy 3:2–3). The importance of this teaching is that
leaders are first and foremost people of good character.
Their example is their biggest message, far above what they
say. We'll talk about this in a later chapter, but high personal
standards are the prime requirement of leaders; the necessary, although insufficient, yardstick.

I shall never forget a colleague of mine describing a
growing tension as he prepared to confront his son about
what he saw as a character weakness. Just before opening his
mouth came the awful realisation that he had the same fault
himself. He snapped his mouth shut and said nothing,
worked on his own weakness and watched his son change
within a couple of years. Sometimes it is a sad thing that as
we influence people, they faithfully copy our weaknesses as
well as our strengths. A similar thing happened with a
member of our local church. She spent much of her time
looking after her grandchildren while her daughter was at
work. Progressively she found both generations headstrong,
stubborn and self-willed. The shock as to the origin of these

traits was not good news. For years she had modelled them to her family!

Now we come to the crunch issue of this chapter:

What do leaders do?

Perhaps more importantly, what should leaders be doing? There are two functions of leadership:

1. Leaders must look after the vision, ie they should spend their time dealing with the broad overview of the long-term future.
2. Leaders must develop the members for whom they are responsible.

Leaders are visionaries

The first issue is summarised in Figure 5.

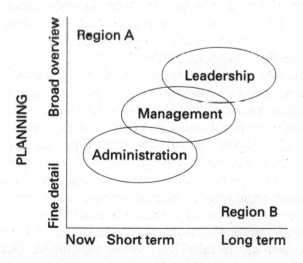

Figure 5. Focus of thinking

The graph plotting time against detail of activity shows that energy should be devoted to the axis from the bottom left of the graph to the top right corner. Don't spend time in region A. The urgency of the short-term requires detailed plans that lead to activity and fruition. No day-dreaming allowed! Region B is equally unproductive and inefficient for leadership. There is no point in drawing up detailed plans applying to a few years away. Our crystal-ball gazing is not good enough (and some of us would refuse to do it!). There will be unforeseen features that we did not predict and nearer the time our detailed plans would have to be redone. Leadership invests time on the vision. Management puts the flesh on the bones and makes plans, which administrators then implement.

I frequently attend meetings of leadership teams and find that very little time is spent on the long-term corporate issues. Most people are more comfortable with short-term scenarios because the results come quickly and give positive feedback. If it can't be done by Monday, it's not worth doing! Hence the bulk of too many leadership meetings focus on crisis management or personal, personnel issues. Whichever description of leaders you prefer, I am certain that long-term thinking is vital to leaders, and while this is more natural to some people than others, to some degree the skill can be developed.

Equally, it is clear that the most popular concept of 'the pastor' has very little to do with leadership, because the focus is on the problems of today, or maybe even yesterday! People issues, unless they focus on development as an interpretation of discipleship, have a short-term time frame.

A good clue in looking for leadership potential is to look for the ability to think across departmental issues, not just the ability to make out a strong case for one department. When it comes to the allocation of resources, leaders have to prioritise between multiple, well-presented, laudable requests. You can only do this against the organisational vision. Good middle managers make good cases for their own departments, but often cannot see, or hear, the validity of parallel claims on the resources.

It is obviously important that all three ovals in the diagram receive attention: we need a vision, strategy and tactical details to be provided by leaders, managers and administrators respectively. If all the time is spent on visionary thinking, there will be plenty of dreaming but no action. If the principal area of concern is the bottom left-hand corner of the diagram, there will be lots of frenetic activity without integration, cohesion and direction. Later, as a result of the lack of purpose, the energy levels will fall. Experientially, I think you will agree that the bigger danger in most organisations is too much activity without cohesion.

'Action, without vision, is just passing the time. Vision, without action, is dreaming' (Joel Barker).

Figure 6 summarises the difference between leaders and managers. Although looking at pairs horizontally is valuable, try to feel the implications of the whole of the left-hand column. That combines to give a picture of the functions of leadership.

Spotting the potential of real leadership is not easy. Sometimes when we first meet emerging leaders, character is sadly lacking. Here are a couple of illustrations about leadership that are very vivid to me. Some years ago, a few students were near to being thrown out of their Bible college. They showed a rebellious streak, they challenged existing practices, they questioned the status quo; in short, they were very uncomfortable to have around. They had a righteous measure of discontent, a feeling that things could be better in their denomination. Now most of them are national leaders in a denomination with which I closely work. They are leading big, growing churches, influencing other pastors and using their people skills wisely. There were many more

Leaders	Managers
Provide vision	Provide goals and realism
Address the process	Address the facts
Focus on concepts	Focus on functions
Look for effectiveness	Look for efficiency
Release potential	Co-ordinate resources
Give direction	Exercise control
Ask 'what?' and 'why?'	Ask 'how?' and 'when?'
Find opportunities	Finish the project
Look at the horizon	Watch the bottom line!
Initiate	Implement
Develop	Sustain
Think about people	Think about structures & procedures
Take the long-term view	Take the short-term perspective
Leadership is a quality	Management is a science

Figure 6. The difference between leaders and managers

placid students at the same college, really 'nice' people, of good character, and never in any trouble with the senior staff. Now they are pastoring small churches, often slowly declining, but in a 'nice' way.

My second example is in a multi-national company. There are various selection procedures to be taken for acceptance to the fast-track graduate development programme. One event is (apparently) a social evening attended by entrants of the last few years. During the informal time, candidates are being assessed on one criterion only: are these people pro-active in their own lives? Do they make things happen or let them happen? In a right way, do they have hopes, ambitions and aspirations? What are they actively doing to work towards them? This company believes that if you cannot be pro-active in your own life, then you will never lead others. They are looking for people who write the future, who have a sense of purpose and destiny. Ambition is important; obviously it can be misused, but the greater danger is having no sense of direction.

Leaders develop their members

There is an old adage about spotting the leaders: all you have to do is to look behind them, because they will have followers. There is something in this theory, but also a major weakness. The ultimate goal of a leader is rather higher and answers the question, 'If anything happened to me tomorrow, would the work continue?' The highest hope of wise leaders is to make themselves redundant.

The last thing leaders want to achieve is dependency.

A leader's ultimate wish is that people will 'do even greater things' than they are doing (John 14:12). We are trying to produce members, not just followers (see figure 7, page 32).

I hope that this book will make a contribution to the second function of leadership, that of developing people who are in our employment or for whom we have a pastoral mandate. I believe that innate within everyone is the desire to grow. If I knew I was going to be subordinate to you for the next five years, I would like the certain knowledge that my character will develop, that the sanctification process will

Leaders	Followers	Members
Lead	Follow	Accompany
Give	Accept	Share
Support	Depend	Belong
Bridge	Walk over	Help each other
Decrease	Exist	Grow

Figure 7.

continue, that my gifts will be utilised, that it will not prove to be one year's experiences five times repeated. True leaders have a track record in these areas that makes them worthy of joining.

In the last decade, many authors contributed to the concept of servant leadership, and when all was said and done, rather more was said than done! The concept is important but often the real implications are misunderstood. I think there were clear reasons for this. First, it's not about washing your disciples feet every day to prove how humble you are. Many people picked up the humility idea, but it should be expressed in how leadership functions are carried out differently, not by reverting to mundane tasks. As the leader, there are certain things that you, and you only, can do; we have described those functions in Figure 6. Secondly, the idea of dying to self appealed greatly as the sort of thing that leaders should say. It tackled the problems of pride and of empire building. But again, very few strategies were offered. What would 'dying to self' look like? What would good leaders do differently? It's about developing people on their terms for the organisation's and individual's benefit. There is not really that much debate about what leaders do; good leaders just do it for different reasons.

The misunderstandings of dying to self and servant leadership might be linked to a final great fallacy about leadership. It is the privilege of membership to be gifted by God and therefore to express those gifts, and leaders are also members. It is not the *function* of leadership to express their gifts. Leaders may seem to have a wide portfolio of gifts, but their primary functional role is to help members express their gifts, and to integrate those contributions for the common good. A passage in Ephesians 4 clarifies the motivation: 'It was he who gave some to be apostles, some to be prophets, some to be evangelists, and some to be pastors and teachers, to prepare God's people for works of service, so that the body of Christ may be built up until we all reach unity in the faith.' (Ephesians 4:11). Gifts have been given for the building up of the body of Christ, not for personal edification. Similarly, the 'higher' role of leaders is to equip others, not simply to do things themselves. That is what dying to self is about.

This article, a scripture plus amplification, illustrates the point:

'I consider that our present sufferings are not worth comparing with the glory that will be revealed in us' (Romans 8:18).

I kept for nearly a year the flask-shaped cocoon of an emperor moth. It is very peculiar in its construction. A narrow opening is left in the neck of the flask, through which the perfect insect forces its way, so that a forsaken cocoon is as entire as one still tenanted, no rupture of the interlacing fibres having taken place. The great disproportion between the means of egress and the size of the imprisoned insect makes one wonder how the exit is ever accomplished at all – and it is never without great labour and difficulty. It is supposed that

*the pressure to which the moth's body is subject
in passing through such a narrow opening is a
provision of nature for forcing the juices into the
vessels of the wings, these being less
developed at the period of emerging from the
chrysalis than they are in other insects.*

*I happened to witness the first efforts of my
prisoned moth to escape from its long
confinement. During a whole forenoon, from
time to time, I watched it patiently striving and
struggling to get out. It never seemed able to
get beyond a certain point, and at last my
patience was exhausted. Very probably the
confining fibres were drier and less elastic than
if the cocoon had been left all winter on its
native heather, as nature meant it to be. At all
events I thought I was wiser and more
compassionate than its Maker, and I resolved to
give it a helping hand. With the point of my
scissors I snipped the confining threads to make
the exit just a little easier, and Lo! Immediately,
and with perfect ease, out crawled my moth
dragging a swollen body and little shrivelled
wings.*

*In vain I watched to see that marvellous
process of expansion in which these silently and
swiftly develop before one's eyes; and as I
traced the exquisite spots and markings of
diverse colours which were all there in
miniature, I longed to see these assume their
due proportions and the creature to appear in
all its perfect beauty, as it is, in truth, one of the
loveliest of its kind. But I looked in vain. My
false tenderness had proved its ruin. It never
was anything but a stunted abortion, crawling*

*painfully through that brief life which it should
have spent flying through the air on rainbow
wings.*

*I have thought of it often, often, when
watching with pitiful eyes those who were
struggling with sorrow, suffering and distress;
and I would fain cut short the discipline and
give deliverance. Short-sighted man! How know
I that one of these pangs or groans could be
spared? The far sighted, perfect love that seeks
the perfection of its object does not weakly
shrink from present, transient suffering. Our
Father's love is too true to be weak. Because he
loves his children, he chastises them that they
may be partakers of his holiness. With this
glorious end in view, he spares not their crying.
Made perfect through sufferings, as the Elder
Brother was, the sons of God are trained up to
obedience and brought to glory through much
tribulation.*

Think back to leaders who have had a significant impact on
you. What appealed to you about them? When I have asked
myself the same question, the common answer is that I knew
that they cared about me and my development, as well as
harnessing my efforts for the good of the organisation.

References

Damazio, Frank, *The Making of a Leader*, revised edition
(Bible Temple Publishing: Portland, Oregan, 1988).

Sproul, R.C., *Stronger than Steel*, twenty-first edition
(Harper and Row: San Francisco, 1939).

Nanus, Burt, *Visionary Leadership* (Jossey-Bass: San
Francisco, 1992).

Greenslade, Philip, *Leadership* (Marshall, Morgan and Scott: Basingstoke, 1984).

Marshall, Tom, *Understanding Leadership* (Sovereign World Ltd.: Chichester, 1991).

Finney, John, *Understanding Leadership* (Daybreak – Darton, Longman and Todd: London, 1989).

CHAPTER 2

THE CORPORATE VALUES AND CULTURE

In the last few years, the importance of values has been widely recognised and explored. I still meet considerable confusion about what values are, and some serious under-estimating of their impact. Values are principles or beliefs which guide decisions and actions. They affect every aspect of life, both personal and corporate, and can be classed under three headings: personal values, product or service values and corporate values.

Let's begin by considering personal values. Two different leaders may list their personal values like this:

Leader A: Approachable, fair minded, supportive, friendly, patient and kind.
Leader B: Committed, diligent, excellent, focused, purposeful and pace-setter.

Their styles will be quite different. Neither is right nor wrong, there is no better and worse. But most of us, in anticipation, know that we would personally have a strong preference to work for one and not the other. A sample of 1,000 readers might vote roughly 500 for each leader.

Values are not the same as beliefs; they come out of our beliefs. The two leaders illustrated above might well have similar beliefs but have very contrasting values. Ideally, our

37

beliefs give rise to our values and our behaviour comes out of our values.

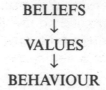

BELIEFS
↓
VALUES
↓
BEHAVIOUR

There may be a gap between our stated, theoretical values and what we actually practise. People around us would find that very disconcerting; at worst we would be accused of lack of integrity. In the long run, our practised values will be much more significant. What we do screams louder than what we say.

Values are caught not taught.

This was the problem that Jesus had with the Pharisees. 'You must obey them and do everything they tell you. But do not do what they do, for they do not practise what they preach' (Matthew 23:3).

The next set of values might be called product or service values. Companies have used the concept as part of their sales strategy. Words like quality, superior and value for money have a ring that entices the customer. More frequently nowadays I am asked for my training values. Ideally, if you attended a residential conference with me, you could write the list for me! They are:

Biblically and experientially based
Modest profile
Tailor made
Competent with the materials
Dedicated.

I can give simple evidences of some, although in action I hope you would see the practical outworking of them all. A modest profile causes me to prefer using a flip chart to an OHP. Dedicated does not mean the same as committed. It means that I am dedicated to each client group for the duration of my courses; there are no mobile phones and I give myself to delegates during meal breaks and informal times. I am contracted lock, stock and barrel. I am using my own work as an example to illustrate the difference between personal and product values. The five features I've listed are consistent with my personal values, but they are not the same thing.

Incidentally, many conflicts occur when there is a clash between the values of the individual and the organisational values. Values don't change easily and issues will crop up regularly based on these value differences. If you are sure that the conflicts are founded on value differences, then things won't get better quickly. There will be a lot of heart searching. After being called to follow Jesus, Peter went through this challenge, where his preconceptions, which were pretty fundamental, had to be faced.

Having briefly considered personal and product values, I want to move on to the crux of the chapter, which is corporate values. Personal values should drive the actions of individuals, corporate values should drive the behaviour within organisations. The concept is the same, it's just the scale that is different. There is evidence in quality management that the corporate culture is the single biggest feature which determines an individual's effectiveness. Surprisingly at first perhaps, the greatest contribution does not come from that person's own efforts. Some researchers indicate that up to ninety per cent is not within their immediate control. It's vital that we understand this before looking at tools for developing leadership. Let's take a couple of vivid examples to illustrate the point.

Many delegates come to time management courses and some are slightly disappointed with the results after trying to implement the principles. They learn about goal setting, priorities, planning, good use of a diary, etc. Why does putting things into practice prove much harder? The corporate culture may be working against the improvements. If most people in the organisation believe in leaving things to the last minute, interrupting each other as soon as they need something, running team meetings badly and operating inefficient systems on e-mail, then improving personal time management is a nightmare. We cannot improve dramatically in isolation.

Similarly, suppose a church conducted a skills and gifts audit to help people find their niche in the church and to become more fulfilled. If historically the minister has done everything, both spiritual and practical, the expectation could now be deeply held, but not stated, that this pattern will continue. There will be no point in identifying the unused gifts of the members if the culture will prevent them from being expressed. Perhaps lip service is paid to full involvement, but there is a gap between the spoken and real values. The outcome is likely to be increased frustration.

Tom Peters, author of many books including *In Search of Excellence*, once said that consultancy on corporate culture was daylight robbery. All he did was go to an organisation and keep his eyes and ears open. It helps if you have devised a little checklist such as figure 8 on page 43. But this masks the difficulty. Most of you would be excellent consultants on corporate culture at any organisation but one – your own! We are so close to the culture of our own church or organisation that we make assumptions and miss the impact of essential ingredients. It's easy to take things for granted. When I've pointed out features as substantial as my two examples, I'm often told, 'Well it's always been like that!' Maybe, but it doesn't alter the impact. Most of the features of corporate culture are taken for granted and rarely questioned. Not only do nations have a culture, but organisations also have a distinctive feel.

For the moment, I am treating culture, climate and ethos as virtually interchangeable. They all roughly mean 'the way we do things here'. The essence of the culture should be the sum of the core values. An organisation might pay more than lip service to fifty values, but give them unequal weight. There will be five or six core values, which have the greatest impact.

I want to summarise the impact that corporate core values have on organisations, whether we recognise or like the fact.

1. Values define the requirements of good relationships.
2. Values focus on how we do things and how people are treated, not on what we do.
3. Values are the responsibility of all managers and leaders.
4. They must be universal and general codes of conduct, and therefore mandatory on all staff, departments and areas of operation.
5. There must be frequent, visible evidence of the core values.
6. Any public statement about core values must focus on the few that summarise your unique ethos.
7. Any differences between stated values and actual behaviour patterns are serious and should be urgently addressed.

The challenge of implementing the values consistently across an organisation is not easy. I see the difficulty vividly when I train managers in residential care work. In the government standards (published in 1986, but recently rewritten in a longer format) there were six core values:

Dignity
Privacy
Choice
Independence
Rights
Fulfilment.

Quite clearly, these were intended to apply to the residents, but I question whether we can really deliver these qualities if we don't apply them to staff as well. The same challenge applies in manufacturing industries: can we really deliver quality goods without treating staff with the same high standards? I doubt it.

Don't forget yourself at this stage. If values are binding across all departments and individuals, you are included in the benefits of good practice. I've known many ministers and senior managers who take care of their staff and clients, but not of themselves. Everybody else must take days off and holidays, but not them. Eventually this won't work. People assume that if it's fine for you, then it's fine for them as well. As we've already said, your actions will speak louder than your words. In some cases, if we love our neighbour as badly as ourselves, it would be a pretty poor example! Probably it comes out of the false concept of servant leadership again.

To help you understand the key ingredients of corporate culture, I've merged two lists devised by researchers, bringing together an American and a European template. Whatever the core values of your organisation, these are key elements of culture. In addition to any others, you are making a statement on these issues and the outcomes will be significant. Some items on the list are drawn from considerations of national cultures, but the dimensions can usefully be applied on a smaller scale, to churches and organisations.

1. Equality

This dimension looks at whether people are regarded equally, and on what basis they are treated unequally. It's usually the status issue. If graduates are preferred, if letters after your name open doors for you, if the old school tie is a powerful message, if the square footage of your office is important, if role has more impact than ability, these would

Figure 8. The core components of the corporate culture

be typical symptoms of a status-driven organisation. Prestige, image and profile are significant.

I visited one missionary society headquarters a couple of years ago. Thirteen doors on the ground floor had nicely engraved plaques on them, starting with the words 'Director of. . . .' I was convinced that the last two would be entitled 'Director of Floor Cleaning Services' and 'Director of Tea and Coffee Making'. It was about the ring of the words, because there was only one person in most of the departments. (Incidentally, the names of the postholders were attached on paper, in pencil; clearly the people were not expected to outlast the posts.)

Over reliance on a uniform or badge of office is along the same lines. I've known this mentality with ex-services personnel. It can be a tiny indicator to me when I visit churches; I've never really known an 'every-member ministry' culture in a church where the minister wears most of their regalia all day, because their clothes are a statement of the position, status and being different. Traffic wardens are capable of the same approach!

If status and prestige are highly important, then it will be very difficult to really emphasise team work, because the essence of status is that it ranks people differently. Culture is closely linked to structure and a hierarchical structure would be strongly adhered to in an organisation that focuses on inequality. It's actually quite hard to develop people in such a setting, for fear of sharing your position.

2. Differentiation between male and female

This feature looks at the differentiation of role between men and women in a society or sub-culture. Given the rapid changes in the role of women in British society, it would be easy to assume that attitudes have permanently shifted but remember that although culture changes slowly as a rule, these attitudes are by no means static. Examples of high role differentiation in developed societies are in Japan and the Middle East at present, closely linked to their different religions. Scandinavian countries tend to treat the sexes very much more equally, as would modern Israel. Obviously, it is not easy to develop women in leadership if your organisational culture accords them very different roles.

3. Interdependence

Britain has moved much more to an independent culture. 'If you haven't got a job, then get on your bike and pedal,' said one politician. Some cultures have a strong sense of responsibility towards the disadvantaged; others are more independent. On a smaller scale, churches and other organisations show wide variations. Interdependence would be characterised by things like teamwork, candour and mutual care.

One result of an interdependent culture is a naturally higher level of communication. Interestingly, Japan has a high interdependence score, which seems to be one of the reasons why quality management was implemented more easily in Japan than in the West. Teamwork was already more common when the process began; fewer managers treated knowledge as a tool to retain power.

4. Proactivity

The contrasting ends of this spectrum vary from 'writing your own future' to 'it's God's will'. The range considers how much an individual within a culture feels in control of their own destiny. Is your future a question of what you make it? The alternative extreme is to see it as a mixture of predetermination and driven features external to your own decision making, for example:

'Well, the boss will pick who he wants';
'I'll let my name be put forward, and if it's right, then I'll be elected.'

If we chose the more fatalistic end of this axis, then we would not recognise the ability to develop leaders. Their progress will be seen as a natural process.

5. Standards

Standards have eventually to be precise and measurable. Without them, we can only surmise how we are doing. Organisationally, standards tell the member the degree to which results are important. In a business situation, these would be more accepted than in a church. There is a small but important distinction to be made at this juncture, since culture and climate are very close. Culture is an objective statement about the organisation; the climate is rather more subjective, more about how the organisation feels, and is therefore more prone to short-term variations. The difference is particularly significant within this dimension. For the manager to say that the required standard is understood is not quite the same as the member saying that they have received the message! It is certainly easier to develop leaders in a culture where standards are accepted, discussed and measured.

6. Order and clarity

It's not enough to have standards; they must also be clearly communicated. This ingredient will be a measure of the effectiveness of the organisation's internal communication, determined principally by the receiver, not the transmitter. But in addition, lines of authority must be known by those using them; systems and procedures must be laid down and communicated. Do people know who to ask when they need help and support?

7. Freedom and conformity

This reflects the degree to which members see themselves bound by rules, policies, procedures and set practices. It also considers how free members are to assert their individuality by reacting against conformity. In many ways, it is the only axis where there isn't one hundred per cent preference about where we would like to be. Superficially, none of us want to breed robots who entirely conform. But when it comes down to health and safety issues, for example, we want people to follow set procedures for the good of everyone. The difficulty is, it is virtually impossible to draw the line where we want conformity and where we would like to encourage initiative and individuality. If an organisation demands too much conformity, it is difficult to develop leaders, largely because mistakes are not tolerated.

8. Risk taking and responsibility

There is a slight similarity between this criterion and the one above; this one views things rather more from the member's perspective. When staff and members do deviate from conformity, do they understand why and how they are doing it? This is a measure indicating membership's perception of making decisions and contributions without constantly having to check with a superior. Over and above this freedom of action lies the response of the subordinate to success and failure when they have acted autonomously. Do they take responsibility for their actions?

9. Rewards

It is not easy to find good methods of rewarding people in the non-profit-making sector, especially in Church life. We can't give them a pay increase and we can't change their 1.6L company car into a 2.0GL! There are only so many ways of saying, 'Well done,' and later on, 'Very well done.' In a later section we will look rather more at what motivates people and will give clearer indications about the rewards that different characters hope for. Certainly, different people understand and expect rewarding in different ways. For some, the 'fear' is that if they do the job too well, then they've got it for life. 'Well done thou good and faithful servant, and as your reward, go and do it again next week!' In some churches, Sunday school teaching works like this. The reward of a job well done is a life sentence! Nevertheless, there are some features about recognition that we ought to understand, especially the components that are critical in the formation of the corporate culture. It's principally about fairness and equity. If two people do a task to a similar standard, then their recognition should be similar in calibre.

10. Team spirit

Team spirit is probably the most frequently discussed dimension of corporate culture, but probably the hardest to define. Essentially we are asking, 'Do the members enjoy themselves?' It is visible and it is fundamental. Laughter, humour and a lightness in the atmosphere are the key hallmarks.

Here is a list of values that I have found publicly stated by organisations that I have visited:

Caring	Releasing talents
Excellence	The value of each individual
Co-operative	Prayerful
Fairness	Consistency in decisions
Partnership	Relational
Accepting	Integrity
Supportive	Forgiving
Encouraging	Family orientated
Innovative	Creative
Relevant	Disagree without fear
Safety	Treat people individually
Meaningful activities	Managers serve employees
Freedom to make mistakes	Honesty
Empathy	Listening
Punctual	Friendly
Fun	Dynamic

Action

1. Write down a list of five or six single words or very short phrases that summarise your personal core values.
2. Make a longer list reflecting the values of your church or organisation. Include a comment or score about each of the ten features listed above. Are there any other significant elements of your corporate culture?
3. Narrow this list down to five or six items which most fully describe your culture.
4. Share this list with your co-leaders. Discuss which features of your corporate culture contribute to a mentality of people development, and which hinder.

References

Ward, Michael, *Why your corporate culture change isn't working . . . and What to do about it* (Gower: Aldershot, 1994).

Hofstede, Geert, *Culture's Consequences*, abridged edition (Sage Publications: London, 1980).

Hofstede, Geert, *Cultures and Organisations: Software of the Mind* (McGraw-Hill Book Company: London, 1991).

Tools for Leaders

MANAGING THE TEMPTATIONS OF LEADERSHIP

Learning to recognise and handle temptation is foundational to effective leadership. It is sometimes easy to forget that, in his humanity, Jesus faced similar temptations to the ones that leaders face today. Further than that, in substance he experienced all the general areas of temptation where we are inclined to fall. A study of the end of Matthew 3 and the first eleven verses of Matthew 4 will pay good dividends. Many of the temptations revolve around character issues, but I am going to focus on the leadership applications here.

Matthew 3:13–4:11

Then Jesus came from Galilee to the Jordan to be baptised by John. But John tried to deter him, saying, 'I need to be baptised by you, and do you come to me?'

Jesus replied, 'Let it be so now; it is proper for us to do this to fulfil all righteousness.' Then John consented.

As soon as Jesus was baptised, he went up out of the water. At that moment heaven was opened, and he saw the spirit of God descending like a dove and lighting on him. And a voice from heaven said, 'This is my Son, whom I love; with him I am well pleased.'

Then Jesus was led by the Spirit into the desert to be

tempted by the devil. After fasting for forty days and forty nights, he was hungry. The tempter came to him and said, 'If you are the Son of God, tell these stones to become bread.'

Jesus answered, 'It is written. "Man shall not live on bread alone, but on every word that comes from the mouth of God."'

Then the devil took him to the holy city and had him stand on the highest point of the temple. 'If you are the Son of God,' he said, 'throw yourself down, for it is written: "He will command his angels concerning you, and they will lift you up in their hands, so that you will not strike your foot against a stone."'

Jesus answered him, 'It is also written: "Do not put the Lord your God to the test."'

Again, the devil took him to a very high mountain and showed him all the kingdoms of the world and their splendour. 'All this I will give you,' he said, 'if you will bow down and worship me.'

Jesus said to him, 'Away from me, Satan! For it is written: "Worship the Lord your God, and serve him only."'

Then the devil left him, and angels came and attended him.

It's OK to be tempted

The Spirit led Jesus into the desert to be tempted. The clear message is that it is all right to be tempted. Leaders are tempted just as much as members; it's just that not only do they face general human issues, but also the testing that comes out of the specific functions of leadership. Leaders are also just as capable of confusing temptation and sin. Certainly our effectiveness will be diminished if temptation leads immediately to guilt or condemnation. There are times when conviction and condemnation start off producing similar knowledge, but they eventually produce very different results. To face temptation and reject it will strengthen us. James 1:2 tells us to 'consider it pure joy . . . whenever you face trials of many kinds' which has always struck me as a little bit of creative accounting, because I seldom feel like that at the time! So part of leadership development is knowing where we are vulnerable, sharpening the recognition of temptation, and resisting better.

Ephesians 6 teaches us about the armour of God. Most of it is defensive, only the sword is an offensive weapon. The shield of faith, however, can be swung into position to meet the enemy in whatever direction is necessary. But if we have an Achilles' heel, then that's what the tempter will go for. There is no point in hammering away at the shield of faith when there is a simple route in. This realisation puts an obligation and responsibility on us to know and recognise our suspect areas. In helping other potential leaders in their development, it is vital that we also help them to recognise the areas in which they are prone to temptation.

Let's note that the temptations for Jesus that are explicitly recorded in the Gospels are here, right at the beginning of his ministry, and in the garden of Gethsemane. Many human leaders are caught unaware part way through their ministry. I firmly believe that the call to leadership can be over glamorised and that we don't prepare people properly for what they will face. Neither do we sufficiently encourage folk to know themselves, which would give them some warning of the temptations that will be peculiar to them.

Additionally, there will be dangers lurking among our strengths. I was with one group of leaders who were discussing each other's strengths and weaknesses. The unanimous opinion was that one fellow's greatest strength was his sense of humour. He is perhaps the best purveyor of one-line jokes that I've ever met. His biggest weakness? His ability to crack a joke at the wrong moment, to spoil a precious discussion, and to draw attention to himself. Both his greatest strengths and biggest weaknesses revolve around his sense of humour.

I can also illustrate the point on a personal level. Objective, critical thinking is a vital contribution to good teamwork. That's my strength. But it can easily drift into a destructive mode, or at least be misinterpreted that way. Critical thinkers see the difficulties and potential dangers easily and often accurately, but can sound negative. Our strengths and weaknesses usually arise out of the same features.

It is important to recognise to which side of a balanced position we are more prone to fall. For example, around the middle position of a diligent leader, the two danger sides are the lazy person and the workaholic. One side only is likely to attract you; if you are hard working by nature, the temptation is usually to think that you are not working hard enough. The lazy person probably thinks that they are working too hard already. Similarly, there is a balanced position on the issue of how much leaders should consult with members. The leader who thinks that they are consulting enough is probably quite autocratic; the one who is worried about riding roughshod over people probably involves them sufficiently already, and needs to be more decisive. Please go back to the functions of leaders and managers (figure 6 on page 30) and identify which function you prefer. It would be a temptation to your leadership if you are too prone to management functions.

The root of all temptation is to break the relationship with the Father

The nub of all the temptations to Jesus was to break his relationship with the Father. The last verse of Matthew 3 is a complete affirmation: 'This is my Son, whom I love; with him I am well pleased' (Matthew 3:17). This would be understandable for most of us after the ascension, or even after the resurrection. After completing his tasks on earth, a statement like 'you've done a good job' would be very much in order. But the affirmation of the Father was before Jesus had done anything! His love was quite independent of success in the task. All the temptations would have involved a detour from the plans of the Father, and for Jesus doing the Father's will was paramount: 'My food is to do the will of him who sent me and to finish his work' (John 4:34). He, who had all power, authority and choice, laid down vested interests because the alternative would have broken the relationship with the almighty.

The temptation to relate worth and work

That's precisely the temptation that faces leaders today. It would be great to just make a small contribution of our own to our salvation. Out of a gratefulness for all God has done for us, the desire to contribute over and above that which he gives us to do is very strong. Before long, we are trying to collect heavenly air miles towards our upward ticket. It is demeaning of the fullness of the package of salvation. My unworthiness is that Christ had to die for me. My worthiness is that he did.

My salvation does not depend on my good works. It's free. Admittedly, some understanding of Christ's lordship requires that I dedicate my life to him afterwards, but that comes out of a heart desire, not a negotiated contribution to the package of salvation. The association of work and worth is a temptation to break relationship with him, in that it undervalues the final price that he paid for us. There are big issues of personal security here and central is the realisation that it is possible to do apparently spiritual works in the flesh. The fact that an activity looks godly does not give us a mandate to do it. The temptation is to undertake too much because we need the feel-good factor.

The temptation to try to please others

This is a very easy trap to fall into. Many people in leadership know the desire to please others; it often goes along with a wrong understanding of servant leadership. We can soon take that further into the trap of jumping through hoops. The members set hoops for the leader to jump through and the leader, believing that this is the way to acceptance, jumps. Sadly there is always another hoop to jump through next week, or worse, as this type of member has a short memory, the same hoop will be there again. The whole danger is based around meeting the expectations of others. 'Do it my way!'

If they don't accept you for who you are, they won't accept you for what you do.

Yet it is very easy to believe the essence of this temptation. We know, in our heads, that we cannot earn respect by our deeds, but it is quite another thing to resist this in the day-to-day grind. It always feels as if with just a little more effort we'll be there, as popular as can be. May I suggest that if we measure ourselves by our works, we are likely to judge others by the same criteria.

One of the most frequent outcomes of this temptation concerns pastoral visiting. Often members want to be visited by the minister; no other visit counts. Another lay person from the pastoral team does not constitute a proper visit. But your gifts might be different and you might interpret the job differently. The temptation is to seek popularity by doing what they expect.

The temptation to self-vindicate

It might be more accurate to say 'to try and self-vindicate!'
I've frequently seen it, including when people leave secular
employment and start full-time ministry. The complication
of balancing work and church is over and now there is a
single-mindedness. But sometimes there is the desire to be
seen to be worth the salary. Suddenly there is the need to do
everything, look busy . . . the congregation is watching. This
drives the temptation for the leader to try and do it all themselves. It's very hard to retain the principle of aiming to
become redundant while wanting to self-vindicate. I've seen
numerous examples of the true quality of Church life going
backwards, immediately after a leader has given up secular
employment. Sometimes this temptation can come from
both the above causes; associating worth with work *and*
trying to please others!

One curate I met managed to do the opposite. The
expectations of the people were pastoral care and visiting
but he was a computer buff. He told me that the parish
weekend had taken three solid weeks to prepare. Partly
because he admitted to having time management problems, I
asked where the hours had gone. Amongst other parts of the
task, this perfectionist had put the room list on computer,
and personally collated and stapled a list for every delegate!

The temptation to do it in my own strength

This is a big one for the multi-gifted, all-singing and all-
dancing leader. I can do it myself, well, at least I can with
God's help. But God was fully human in Christ and we, as
leaders, are made in his image, not as the new improved latest
model. Jesus was capable of acknowledging his needs, and
the message is that we must be able to do the same. It is stated
clearly when he was hungry, thirsty or tired. Leaders seem to

be reluctant to admit to having needs, as though their image will be tarnished. This leads very quickly to a loss of reality, even if it is apparently based on a desire not to burden others with our problems. We all know the plastic sound of 'How are you today?' 'Oh, I'm fine!' when blatantly everything is not.

Leaders will always have demands made on them to provide support and help for others, but they must also learn to allow others to minister to them. Jesus had an inner team of three, of whom more was asked as well as further opportunities offered. There was no difficulty about this for the other nine disciples. The only bickering we read about was from Mrs Zebedee, wanting the two best seats in the kingdom for her sons. There are no recorded problems between the outer nine disciples and the inner team. I think leaders today are sometimes reluctant to form deep relationships because of the danger of appearing to show favouritism. Leadership can be a very lonely business so I want to encourage you to build friendships, both within your own church or organisation, and with external contacts.

The temptation to go for the quick fix

The temptation to jump down from the temple and do something miraculous must have been a big test for Jesus. No pain, the media would have wanted interviews in no time, and he would quickly earn mass publicity. Apart from this not being God's chosen method, most quick-fix solutions aren't all they appear to be from the outside. If it really is that simple, it would have been done before. Progress is not like buying a car tyre; not all advertised prices are subject to discounts. There is a real danger in presenting an over-glamorous concept of leadership without being honest and open about the costs involved. Neither cheap fixes nor quick impacts produce lasting fruit in isolation from more costly inputs.

The temptation to use power for my own needs

All the old clichés spring quickly to mind. 'Power corrupts, and absolute power corrupts absolutely.' Or, depending on your point of view, it could be rewritten: 'Power corrupts, and absolute power is absolutely wonderful!'

I'm using the term 'power' loosely here, but the temptation to Jesus was to use what he had for his own agenda. The message is that today's leaders face the same trials, the same temptations to manipulate for their own purposes. Accountability is not always sought and dying to self is the daily challenge. Again, baby and bath water go together. The temptation is rooted in the same skills and drives that make the leader effective.

The temptation to quit

In periods of difficulty, I guess most leaders must ask them-selves whether it's all worth the candle. There's an honest recognition of the cost of ministry, both personally and often to the family as well. Jesus knew the cost as well as any of us. He must have wondered about the alternatives, espe-cially as he set his face towards Jerusalem. Even when we are clear about the call of duty, when we know what is the right path, it's seldom straight and smooth. Reported stress in leaders has rocketed. The rate of increase in divorce among Christian leadership is one of the highest among Europe's professional occupations. Again, I think we have a clear duty to prepare people realistically, because the temptation to deviate from the path will be very real.

The temptation to avoid making decisions

Sometimes there are difficult decisions to be made in leader-ship – the sort where whatever you decide, someone will dis-agree and might take offence. The more relationships matter to us, the more difficult it is to decide in these situations. Even in less tricky circumstances, the desire to please people may result in wrong decisions, or often, no decision at all, for fear of offending. The temptation to cloud decision-making with over-sensitivity is common and can come from the best of intentions. Anything for a quiet life! The best answer lies in being part of a team, where collective decisions remove some of the temptation to focus on individuals rather than the common good.

Practical hints

1. Be honest with God, yourself and others. It's the core of the meaning of integrity.
2. Know the overall direction that you believe your organisation should take and constantly check whether programmes and activities are consistent with this direction.
3. Consider the ways in which you, as a leader, can be accountable.
4. How much of your delegating is for the development of others, as opposed to just getting the job done?
5. Who are your true friends? Increase the number of hours you spend with them.
6. When you last worked too many hours in a given week, were you secretly pleased or disappointed?
7. What was the last temptation that you recognised and repulsed?
8. Is your relationship with God stronger now than at the beginning of your ministry?
9. Are the main aspirations that you hold for the organisation likely to be fulfilled within the next six months? If so, seek longer vision.
10. Can I recall taking the easy option for a quiet life? Why did I choose this path?

As with all the tools in this book, remember the twin applications. I hope this section has caused you to be more aware of your own temptations as a leader, but the last section of ten hints and questions might well be useful to work through in a development time as you try to help other potential leaders.

My temptations in leadership

Here are some temptations listed by delegates from leadership conferences that I have been involved in during recent years. They are related to public role rather than personal life. Please tick up to eight of these temptations which you recognise as areas where you are frequently tested. If any really stand out, then mark them with a double tick.

1. To try to prove myself to others ____
2. To deny my responsibilities ____
3. To take short cuts ____
4. To lose sight of my objectives ____
5. To rely on my own strength ____
6. To deny my personal needs ____
7. To try to avoid paying the cost ____
8. To set wrong priorities ____
9. To use my position for my own ends ____
10. To be wrongly swayed by the views of others ____
11. To aim for the dramatic or sensational ____
12. To behave differently, varying between public and private life ____
13. To give it all up ____
14. To be self-centred ____
15. To opt for personal comfort ____
16. To look for reassurance ____
17. To be emotionally self-sufficient ____
18. To try to impress ____

19. To step outside the boundaries of my authority ____
20. To take personal pride in my achievements ____
21. To neglect my personal devotional time ____
22. To act first and count the cost later ____
23. To doubt my call ____
24. To embellish the story ____
25. To relate personal worth to success and failure ____
26. To take my identity from my role ____
27. To deviate through frustration ____
28. To forget that God provides ____
29. To deny others the space to grow ____
30. To be driven by financial concerns ____
31. To impose solutions on others ____
32. To put off the unpleasant tasks ____
33. To please the passengers ____
34. To bend the rules ____
35. To show partiality ____
36. To skip quality time with others ____
37. To retreat to comfort zones to avoid people ____
38. To achieve the task at the expense of people ____
39. To put off the task to a more 'suitable' time ____
40. To be the 'miracle worker', making myself
    the answer ____
41. To cut corners ____
42. To try to do it all myself ____
43. To be obstinate for obstinacy's sake ____
44. To choose poor solutions because of time
    pressures ____
45. To expect others to act for you ____
46. To cut corners in preparation ____
47. To duck confrontation ____
48. To put off the hard, unpopular decision ____
49. To try to gain popularity ____
50. Any others? ____

Action

1. List your most frequent temptations. Can you see any common root or similarities?
2. Write down one thing that you can do to spot the 'onset' of each.
3. Write down one thing that you can do to minimise the impact of each.
4. Work through this exercise again with the other members of your team.
5. Share your results with each other.
6. Constantly remember that his grace is sufficient!

EXPLORING MOTIVES

To recognise what motivates people can often provide the key to understanding their behaviour and give major indications about their future development. It's right but limited to say that we are motivated by the love of God. Although the statement has an absolute quality it fails to take account of the variations about how that love could be experienced and expressed. The concepts and language used by managers and leaders to provide motivation is no more constructive: it revolves around the 'better pep talk' mentality. The truth is that motivation comes from within; it's not something that you can give to people. You can take a horse to water, but you cannot make it drink. Good leaders recognise that they are basically good situation managers, providing appropriate opportunities, and knowing that *different people are motivated by different opportunities*. One scenario will not equally excite a range of people.

Research indicates that thought patterns are central to motivation. The more we dwell on something, the more likely we are to do it. 'For as he thinks in his heart, so is he' (Proverbs 23:7, Revised Authorised Version). It is as though we have a series of mini-cassette recorders inside our heads. In some cases, we are familiar with the music, we know where the tape is to be found and the switch requires a very light touch. Above all, we enjoy the music. Other tapes are less familiar and we don't want to play them so much. We all have a full range of tapes inside, but we have established patterns of choice. There are other features that have a bearing on what motivates us, for example, our value system. I saw a bright red Porsche yesterday; and by extending my mortgage I could buy one. The music of the tape is familiar, but my value system says that this expenditure would not be wise so I do not turn the thought process into action. And finally, when science has had its say, there is the less predictable and less rational component, which is how we feel on a given day. In summary:

A MOTIVE IS: A THOUGHT PATTERN
PLUS VALUES
PLUS FEELINGS
which leads to ENERGISED
BEHAVIOUR.

The last line of this definition is important, as it rules out the concept of duty, obligation and commitment. Motivation is about excitement and pleasure, not drudgery or commitment.

The sustained research of David McClelland has involved over 3 million people. He identifies more than 100 motives but *three* dominate. They are called the *primary social motives* and between them they account for about ninety-five per cent of thinking and activity. Food, oxygen in our lungs and fluids are motivational forces, but for most of us they are readily available so they do not dominate our thinking. Sometimes we might use the word 'drives' interchangeably with motives.

Perhaps more provocatively, McClelland claims that an individual's profile is established roughly by fourteen to fifteen years old. The formative process of our early years exposes us to the potential of the different tapes and we form choice patterns and establish preferences. As a Christian, I have had to work through and challenge this concept, but I am now convinced of its validity. I put my motive profile under different sovereignty when I became a Christian, but I don't believe that my personality was torn up at salvation. If we read about characters like Peter and Paul, where we have comments about them both pre and post salvation, we find a great similarity between the types of situation which energised them in both states. While we all have a measure of all three primary social motives,

About sixty-five per cent of the population are much stronger in one drive than the other two.
Roughly thirty per cent are much stronger in two drives than the third.
Less than five per cent have similar levels in all three drives.

Bear in mind that it does not make people more 'balanced' to be high in all three motives. In fact, three high drives is a very difficult profile to live with. With all profiles, the important thing is that the job or context (what is demanded of me), fits who I am. The energy triggered will be some function of the motive profile of the person combined with the situation. A counter example selected fifty people who were easily animated by relationships and put them to work, solo, as lighthouse keepers. The context was so demotivating that nobody lasted more than seventy-two hours before forgetting to do the only thing that they were supposed to do – switch on the light! By any standard, they were highly motivated people, but not by that situation.

At this stage it would be good to remember that pay is *not* a motivator. If you pay me twice as much I won't work twice as hard. But the absence of pay is a demotivator. Pay is a necessary but not a sufficient condition for motivation to be aroused. Both Maslow and Hertzberg made significant contributions to our knowledge of motivation before McClelland's work, including looking at these subjects.

We now need to describe the three *primary social motives* and understand the work patterns that will be appreciated by people strongly motivated in the different drives. Remember that the names of the drives are being used technically, and do not entirely conform to the usual dictionary definition. McClelland actually wrote the letter 'n' in front each title, both to indicate 'the need for' but also to show that the words were being used in a non-standard manner. He has spent some time wishing that he had used less evocative terms that would not produce such strongly held preconceptions.

The three primary social motives are called the need for *achievement, affiliation* and *power*. I want to summarise some of the key features in tabular form (see figure 9 on page 70).

These three main drives are true world wide; the research was conducted in nineteen different countries and the results are completely asexual. Remember that these primary social motives affect everything that we do, our work preferences, hobbies, what we think, the style of leadership that we prefer using, the vocabulary we use and our approach to relationships. Let me now give you three cameo stories, each written as purely as I can in the language of one particular motive. As you read the sketches, try to spot the correct motive:

Scenario 1

'What did you do at the weekend, Bryn?'

'I went to my son's football match. John's parents came along, nice couple. And you know Dave who broke his ankle last week? Well, we've all signed a card for him and I'm going to drop it round to his home on Monday. Oh, and the kids looked great together in their new kit.'

'What was the score?'

'Well, we won, but that's not important. It's the teamwork that matters, win, draw or lose.'

	ACHIEVEMENT	AFFILIATION	POWER
Preferences at work and other general characteristics	Task focused Working alone High standards Clear challenge Moderate risk targets Results dependent on own efforts Personal accomplishments Like making improvements Efficient Technically competent	Team working Relationships Interpersonally sensitive Supportive Empathetic Wide friendships Inoffensive Especially want to be liked Keep in touch	Helping, advising Counselling Initiating, changing Persuading Influencing Need status Extreme risks, high or low Like to make an impact Interpersonally skilled
Typical job situations	Conveyancing solicitor Accountant Engineer Pilot Car mechanic WP operator	Reception class teacher GP in a small rural practice Relatively mundane jobs done together Receptionist Many jobs where the focus is teamwork	Teaching adults Delegating Managing people Barrister (persuading) Public speaking Actor
Preferred leadership styles	Pace-setter Goal maker	Personal Democratic	Directive Coaching
Leisure time	DIY Reading Musical soloist Non-team sports	Clubs, societies Hospitality Anything with lots of people!	Debate Arousing emotion Organising people Coaching
Reaction to feedback	Like lots of feedback Keep it objective and task focused	They blush in response to praise or criticism! They hear 'you don't love me any more' in any negatives	Extreme reactions: Positive feedback: Might produce magnificent response Negative feedback: Argue the toss

Figure 9

Scenario 2

'What did you do at the weekend, Bryn?'

'I went to my son's football match.'

'How did it go?'

'Hammered them, four nil. The centre forward has sixteen goals already this season, and it's not the end of October yet. At this rate, we could be certain of promotion by March, never been done before. Perhaps the first championship ever settled before Easter. The keeper hasn't let in a goal for 173 minutes now.'

Scenario 3

'What did you do at the weekend, Bryn?'

'I went to my son's football match.'

'How did it go?'

'For crying out loud, don't talk to me about Saturday. If the kids are going to play properly, they've got to have linesmen who can keep up with the play. I'm sick of these wellington boots and overcoats. All games for twelve-year-olds and above need three full officials. I've written to the local FA about it, and if that doesn't work, I'll write to Glen Hoddle. They deserve a fair deal.'

(Answers at the end of the chapter.)

It is quite possible that all three scenarios were describing the same football match. Different people see different things and reckon different highlights are worth recording. The Gospels show this very well. John was high in affiliation motivation. Among many other indications, only John has the 'long discourse' section of teaching (chapters 14 to 17), the only record that Peter went out and wept bitterly after the denials, and the only mention of the restitution on the shores of the Sea of Galilee. There are no deliverance examples in John, only a general reference to the work of Beelzebub. Those were not the type of conflicts that he deemed worth recording. Paul's language is a great contrast. Galatians is strong in achievement language and Romans is principally power imagery. John was high in one motive whereas Paul was high in both achievement and power.

There are two principal sources of confusion as you begin to use this excellent tool. First, be careful not to jump to conclusions when you meet people who thrive on relationships with others; their satisfaction might come out of either the power or affiliation drives. When Paul writes that he longs to be with people, he comes with an agenda, the desire to change things. That's the power drive. People high in power motivation need people around them just as much as affiliators, but to influence them, not just to be with them.

Secondly, the presence of high standards does not necessarily mean achievement motivation is the force. 'I pass examinations' is a statement about achievement, but 'I teach others to pass exams' is power imagery. 'We enjoy working together' reflects the need for affiliation. Seldom is the activity the full indicator; why people enjoy the activity and what they get out of it are much more significant. For example, I could have listed fell-walking as a typical achiever's hobby, but this is only a stereotype. Look at these three statements, in the same way as the football stories:

'I always like to climb the highest mountain in the area.'
'I like climbing mountains with my friends.'
'One day, I want to be photographed with Chris
    Bonnington on the top of a mountain.'

The first is an achievement message, the second is about affiliation and the final one reflects the power drive, being with influential, successful people. All the statements reflected an enjoyment of fell-walking, but enjoying it for different reasons.

Each of the drives has its attendant strengths and weaknesses that have to be managed. These are predictable and will not go away. Here are some of the typical features associated with each motive:

MOTIVE	STRENGTHS	POSSIBLE WEAKNESSES

ACHIEVEMENT	Diligent
	Results and goal
	  orientated
	Task orientated
	Practical
	Realistic
	High standards
		Low
		  communication
		  skills
		'Workaholic'
		Poor delegator
		Perfectionist
		Misses the
		  benefits of
		  team play

AFFILIATION	Warm
	Friendly
	Supportive
	Sensitive
		Avoids
		  confrontation
		Cannot work
		  alone
		Too sensitive
		Too many
		  meetings!

POWER	Good delegation
	Enabling
	Can get results
	  through others
	A shaker and
	  mover
		Manipulation
		Domination
		Controlling
		Lack of
		  sensitivity

Figure 10

As I said at the beginning of this chapter, there is no such thing as a good or bad profile. What matters is, can we put square pegs in square holes and round pegs in round holes? Sometimes it's not so much changing the task as changing the manner of doing it. Putting an achiever on the coffee rota for the refreshments after the service by themselves is fine, but not for an affiliator – unless they can serve it, in which case expect long queues! They may make excellent coffee, but would prefer to work in pairs. Making coffee is not particularly exciting but building relationships meets their needs and gets the coffee made.

Nevertheless, sometimes there are serious differences between the profile of the person and the requirements of the task. I've often found this with secretaries to church leaders. The role is principally about typing, filing and other office duties, especially suitable for somebody who is high in achievement motivation. There is very little people interaction. At the interviews, a bright, smiling, friendly person is recruited with a comment like, 'Oh, they will make a great contribution to the team!' We are selecting according to the wrong criteria; we have probably found an affiliator. The outcome is usually a secretary desperate for people contact during work hours, the office work falling behind schedule, plus a large phone bill. If the role was largely as a receptionist, the affiliator would be much more fulfilled.

This is not to say that we are incapable of doing things that require a different profile. We can, provided that the 'distortion' is not too severe or sustained. For example, my profile is highest in power and lowest in affiliation. Suppose I come home from work and my wife reminds me that there is a church social event that evening. The expectation is that affiliation motivation is the requirement, so having arrived at the party, I act outside my natural profile. Initially I dutifully offer sandwiches, fill glasses, and politely ask about the family, but progressively I find that I'm not really listening carefully to the answers. Then somebody says, 'Bryn, I know this is a social evening, but I've got a problem at work and wonder if we could chat about it for a few minutes?' The situation has changed, my power drive engages and I can comfortably use it in helping them. I only hope that it is a really interesting and complex problem!

This artificial distortion of our natural profile is called arousal and suppression. We can do it for a limited period, with some discomfort, but not on a sustained basis. Many people who are low in power motivation find conflict very uncomfortable in a similar way; sometimes the reason for over-reacting is because the situation is so unpleasant that they want the confrontation finished as soon as possible.

I am very aware that the information in this section does not leave you equipped to score profiles accurately. The full tests cannot be marked and scored by yourself because they do not involve just ticking boxes. However, they do access both the objective and subjective parts of the brain. But it is not critical to be able to score precisely; the general high and low scores will tell you something about what situations will help people to 'light their own fire'. Let's summarise some of the potential indicators:

1. What aspects of their work do they really enjoy? Why do they enjoy these parts of the job? Be careful of high-lighting tasks done out of a sense of duty or obligation.
2. What do they do with their leisure time? Again probe further, either by observation or discussion, to find out why they enjoy certain activities. Remember the examples that we have looked at already, you can climb mountains or go to football matches for a variety of reasons.
3. How much do they need the presence of other people around them? Affiliators need people for friendship, power folk need others to influence them or impress them, and achievers are often content with their own company.
4. Look for hints from bookshelves and office walls. Affiliators would have informal pictures of family and friends, achievers would chose manuals, graphs of results and certificates. Power people could have a variety of items but you would certainly notice them!
5. McClelland's classic method of informally identifying

motive profiles is to give people feedback. I've outlined the typical potential responses earlier in the chapter.

6. How important are results, standards and challenge? If they are a regular feature of interest and importance, the person will not be an affiliator. To split the other two drives, note who is responsible for implementation. Achievers do things themselves, power people get others to do them.

7. This is a good time to refer back to the last chapter where we looked at helping people to manage their temptations. We can gain clues about the motive profiles of those we are trying to develop by looking at their typical temptations. Try to match the 'weaknesses' column in the last diagram with the strongest temptations that you identified in the last chapter. Remember, about one third of the population are high in two drives, can comfortably switch between them, and frequently do.

Finally, let us summarise the type of opportunities which these drives relish.

ACHIEVEMENT MOTIVATION needs:

Clear goals
Results within their own control
Regular feedback
Challenge
Moderate risk situations
Just rewards.

AFFILIATION MOTIVATION needs:

The opportunity to form a wide range of friendships
The chance to listen and affirm
Low requirement to challenge, confront or influence
    others
Teamwork
Acceptance, social events and groups, without a task focus.

POWER MOTIVATION needs:

Opportunities to influence and impress
High or low risk situations
A public profile, status
The knowledge that they have made an impact
Opportunities to help or teach, or to receive help or
    teaching
Situations where co-ordinating and directing are possible

Action

The insights of this section have been the most important tool to me in understanding personality, and I am familiar with a wide range of psychometric tests. The biggest difficulty for you is that the only really accurate assessment methods are not self-scoring. Hence there are dangers, especially as I am saying that profiles are fixed by fifteen years old. Nevertheless, it is vital that you get a realistic understanding of your own motive profile, and an insight into those team members that you are responsible for developing. Use the questions and tables in this section and discuss the conclusions with friends. Above all, be honest; we are interested in what excites us, not what we think should excite us!

Answers to the three scenarios: affiliation, achievement and power (in that order).

References

New and Cormack, *Why Did I Do That?* (Hodder and Stoughton: London, 1997).
McClelland, David C., *Human Motivation* (Cambridge University Press: Cambridge, 1987).

TOOL 3

IDENTIFYING KEY RESULT AREAS

Key result areas are the life-blood of time management. Without them, it's virtually impossible to make time management tools work. We will need to do a sketch of the whole subject of time management before reaching this practical and precious nugget.

There are two good reasons for constantly wanting to improve our time management, first to be more effective and secondly to reduce stress. This is not a book about stress management, so I will only briefly refer to the subject. Developing leadership is partly about helping others to manage stress better. Too often, stress management seems to be about shooting yourself in the foot and then learning how to walk again. Prevention is obviously better than cure. The two biggest stressors are poor time management and poor change management, so anything that we can do to manage time better will reduce unnecessary stress.

When I first became involved in training work, I spent one summer reading all that I could on time management, about twenty books. Whether that was good use of my time is another question! After finishing the first few books, I found no new principles, and there have been no fresh revelations in the couple of books that I have scanned each year since then. That's not really surprising, since the principles are as old as time itself. They are all outlined in Genesis 1. But, having said that the concepts haven't changed, the application has not become any easier. Time management is often the first component required in leadership training and it is still the day of training that I am most often asked to provide. Again, there is a logic to this. I like to think of 'time management' as 'managing myself', and if a manager cannot do that, then he is in no position to lead others. Self-management is the basic building block.

Here are my basic premises for time management

1. *There are enough hours in the day.*

Without this premise, the section really would have to become a study of stress management. God equips those whom he calls and his provision includes sufficient hours.

2. *You will have to make some tough decisions.*

You are the most important stakeholder in the use of your time. One day you will be held as accountable for it as for your use of finance. Nobody else is aware of all the variables, not your boss, spouse, children, minister or anybody else, so the big decisions are down to you.

3. *Accept and balance the four life domains.*

I suggest that there are four main domains of our lives:

Work
Church
Family
Personal.

These four have to be kept in balance. It's acceptable to skew the distribution of time across these four unevenly for a season, but not for more than about six months. We can all operate out of balance for some special need, but it is downright unhealthy to ignore any one of these facets for too long. When work and church become one, things sound as though they ought to become simpler. Sadly, too often the family and personal domains also become part of the same facet and Jack becomes a dull boy. 'My work is my hobby' is a dreadful statement on the quality of life and often on the ability to build and sustain relationships. Many leaders who treat work, church, family and leisure as the same endanger the family. There are tools for prioritising within a domain, but there is no 'tool' to serve us across the domains.

4. *Recognise the difference between effective and efficient.*

Effectiveness means:	Doing the right things.	Answering the question 'What?'
Efficiency means:	Doing things right.	Answering the question 'How?'

The obvious danger is that we become very efficient at doing the wrong things. I promise you that if your time management is creaking under the pressures imposed on it, then the answers will lie in your effectiveness, not in your efficiency. We make the bulk of efficiency savings quite automatically. You cannot read a book that much faster, you cannot shorten the phone call much more without being rude, you cannot drive across town much faster, at least not legally! The question is whether we should read that book, make that call or drive across town at all.

5. *Recognise the other features that determine our effectiveness.*

In this section we are looking at the *personal skills of time management*. But clearly this is not the highest aspiration, it

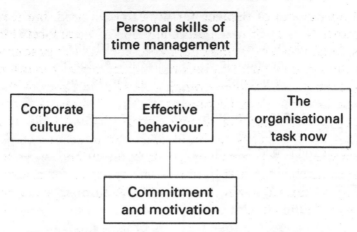

Figure 11. The features that determine our effectiveness

is only a means to an end. The ultimate aim might be the central one in the diagram, effective behaviour. The diagram shows us that there are other things that determine our effectiveness as well as our own skills.

The corporate culture. We have discussed this in chapter 2. Good time management is a team game. There will be ingredients in the corporate culture that have a big impact on individual efforts to master time management.

The organisational task now. Factors which are external to us, but within the organisation, affect our time management. Anything like the youth worker and his family moving away from the area and the church, or a secretary retiring, or an influx of new members from a mission, could alter the work-load of the minister. Any feature that has changed recently will have implications in the job. Reassessment is needed. This is the principal reason why people seem to have time management well under control one day, but twelve months later can be struggling again. The 'job' is never static.

Figure 12. The matrix of motivation and commitment

<u>Commitment and motivation</u>. As we mentioned in the last section, there are better days and worse days. After a holiday, or when a particular project has gone well, we feel that we can tackle anything. On another day, for example if relationships are a little sour, we are not so excited and raising our game is that bit more difficult. Just accept that on bad days you are going to achieve a little less, and address the issues that are causing the problem. I find December notoriously difficult for maximum productivity. Between September and Christmas is usually the most demanding time of the year for training engagements; we can all be a little stale at the end of a busy period of time.

I now want to consider three tools for managing ourselves: goal setting, prioritising and writing a job description.

Goal setting

Quite simply, if you are not happy about setting goals, then time management is impossible. They are also central to the management of change; they are the little cairns on the way to the summit. Goals are not inherently wrong, but there is a great deal of fear about them. I think that there is so much criticism and self-condemnation around that people choose not to set goals. Why? Because I guarantee that if you start setting goals your failure rate will go up. If you never aim for anything you will never have to experience missing targets! However, research has shown quite clearly that if you do set goals you will achieve more. Incidentally, you cannot prioritise dreams, so stating things in goal format is critical to establishing priorities.

Years ago, the phrase 'work smarter, not harder' was very popular. I use the initials of 'smart' to list the following characteristics of goals:

S   pecific
M   easurable
A   ttractive
R   ealistic
T   imed

Specific

If we are going to generate action, we have to narrow the focus of activity. So, for example, it would not be enough to say, 'I'm concerned about relationships in the family at the moment.' A statement like, 'Relationships between myself and my second son are rather strained,' would be more likely to lead to action. Even better would be something like, 'I will do something about the rather strained relationship between myself and my second son.'

Measurable

The real power of goals lies in their measurability. Japanese business leaders say, 'If you can't measure it, you can't manage it.' We may fight shy of measuring many things, but most things can be made measurable by these two questions:

What will there be more of or less of?
How much more or less?

One friend asked me how this could apply to character development. I asked him what he was working on in his own life at the moment. After a pause he stated that he wanted to be a more humble person. I asked what evidence there would be if he succeeded. 'I would interrupt people less often, and try not to finish their sentences for them,' he said. That was measurable. Spiritual? Definitely, for believe me, it was not going to happen without outside assistance!

Attractive

The important thing to remember here is 'attractive to whom?' It must appeal to the person doing the task, not the delegator. I ask my wife to help in many aspects of my work. They are all important and interesting to me, but the actual doing may not be so exciting to her. There is all the difference in the world between agreed tasks and imposed tasks. Whenever possible, discuss and consult; you'll get a far better response.

Realistic

It's good that goals are challenging, but we should never set goals that are doomed to failure before they hit the paper. Risky, yes, challenging, yes, requiring faith, yes, but not impossible please. The desired level of challenge in goals varies for different individuals. Some authors recommend that you should set goals on the basis of expecting about a fifty per cent success rate. I prefer nearer seventy-five per cent, but you can make out a good case that the more you expect to achieve, the higher your overall productivity. Aim high and you won't miss by much! Risk is quite evidently linked to other personality traits, as we saw in the last section.

Timed

Most goal statements either contain a 'by' or 'starting' phrase. The time limit is the part which provides the urgency, otherwise they tend to drag on for ever. We need to state a deadline for completion.

Examples of goal statements:

I will read two chapters per day for a fortnight, starting next Monday.

I will precis the minutes of the council meeting into one side of A4 paper on Thursday evening.

I will read two books on management by Christmas.

Please note that none start with 'I hope to . . .' That is usually insurance policy language, building in excuses for failure before it happens. Also, planning is not part of goal setting: there is no mention of method. The 'how to' comes after the 'what to'. As I said earlier, goal setting is the basic brick in the building called time management. We need to set goals before prioritising. It's just not possible to prioritise dreams and hopes.

Priorities

The next two components were the most practical suggestions put in front of me in the first one-week management course that I attended. First, make a list of your tasks daily. We can only hold one conscious thought, so unclutter your conscious mind by writing things down as they occur to you. Write them in goal format. Do your list at the end of the previous working day. If you leave it till the start of your day, you may well get attacked by people or paper and start doing things that you shouldn't do. Secondly, ask yourself some questions about your priorities. Allocate to each task: A, B or C:

A: Must be done
B: Should be done
C: Could be done.

Obviously, this technique is only useful if all the A tasks are completed each day. If this is not true, there are commonly two reasons. Either you are not controlling interruptions sufficiently, or you are over-optimistic. You should be able to control fifty to sixty per cent of your time in an office type scenario. This means that you should plan about five hours content in a typical working day.

There is still a big hole in the technique mentioned above. Let's suppose that when you return to work tomorrow morning, there are just two jobs on your desk remaining to be done. One is marked 'urgent' and the other is labelled 'not urgent'. You would know which one should be done. The following day, there are again two jobs, one marked 'important' and the other labelled 'not important'. Again, at least you would know which job should be done. Here endeth the humour!

The practicalities are different. There are more than two jobs, they don't arrive already labelled and if they were labelled accurately, some would say 'urgent, but not important' and others would say 'important, but not urgent'. We must analyse urgency and importance separately. Urgent is purely a time-scale question, much as we would find in the dictionary definition of the word. It is not an absolute word, because it depends on how full my diary is. If the next fourteen days of my diary are congested, then an urgent task might still be difficult to finish in the next two weeks. But if today is not pressurised, and you ask for something urgently, then I might be able to do it in the next eight hours. It's all relative.

Important is not a word that we will use in the normal sense. Important to whom? Your partner, yourself, God, your boss, your minister? We will use the word in a specific and different sense.

IMPORTANT means IT DESERVES ME.

I need to do this task. It warrants my unique package of experience, gifts, character and skills. We can summarise these two concepts in the following diagram.

	URGENT	NOT URGENT
IMPORTANT	Do it	Plan to do it
NOT IMPORTANT	Delegate it	Leave it

Figure 13. Urgent and important

This really is the focus of the whole section. For leaders to do the things that they and they only can do, they need to understand the meaning of their job at any given time. 'Important' needs redefining from time to time; without a clear understanding it is impossible to establish priorities. Most people still wrongly make priorities on the basis of urgency instead of both variables.

Writing a job description

Before deciding what can and should be delegated, there needs to be a clear understanding about what a job entails.

Leaders often find this very difficult. It is easy to confuse the reasons for this difficulty. The leadership job is quite stressful but actually there is a great deal of flexibility. There is evening work, but there is no reason to work morning, afternoon and evening in a given day. There are vast variations in the average weekly hours totalled by various ministers, church and mission leaders, as well as in what they do with those hours, so obviously the leadership job is open to wide interpretation.

Job descriptions are becoming more common within the Christian work sector, despite resistance. I think there are two main reasons for this residual unpopularity. First, as in any other sector, if a perceived need is not going to be met, then there is no point in writing a job description. The track record is that too many job descriptions are not worth the paper they are written on. As we saw earlier, the establishing of priorities is the hardest area for many of us. Therefore any worthwhile job description's effectiveness must filter through, and contribute to prioritising; otherwise, there will be no point in writing one. Secondly, the biggest difficulty sometimes comes from an over-spiritual perception of the role. 'I'm accountable to God, brother!' is actually shorthand for 'And to nobody lesser, and certainly not during this life.' Yes, there honestly are situations where the will is the key issue. If you don't want to be accountable, then you will probably find a way of not being accountable.

There are many other good reasons for having a clear understanding of the job. In any caring profession, the difficulty is that the job is never done. That makes it even more important to set some boundaries, enabling us to leave unfinished business with a feel-good factor rather than false guilt. For people in regular secular employment, their work in the church needs boundaries even more, since they have more domains to juggle.

There should be eight components in a practical job

description. Make a genuine effort to describe the job realistically rather than through rose-coloured glasses. Use clear, unambiguous language. I recommend using the following format:

1. The job title

This should be meaningful, accurate and as short as possible. Don't pander to status games, especially if it will not be born out in practice, eg a director would be expected to give direction for the whole organisation, or at least a division. Their accountability would usually be to a Chief Executive or a Director General. So managers are expected to manage, advisors should advise, assistants should assist, and administrators should administrate. We also need to be clear about the specific meaning of these terms within our organisation.

2. The purpose of the job

This is a succinct statement setting out what the job is for. Why does it exist? What is its core aim? What is the post-holder intended to achieve? For example:

To provide leadership for. . . .
To provide secretarial support for. . . .
To manage the financial information systems in
    accordance with. . . .
To meet the pastoral needs of. . . .

If there are two or more quite distinct parts they should be addressed separately. A shared secretary could be an example of the need for a twin purpose statement. But at this second stage, keep to the overview; no more than one sentence per role.

3. Accountability

To whom is this post-holder accountable? This formally provides an answer to the question, 'Who is my boss?' The church administrator must know whether he or she is answerable to the minister, wardens, diaconate, etc. Secretaries to more than one boss find themselves in difficult situations unless this is made clear. For work to have a sense of direction, we all need to know what our priorities are, and who to refer to over major issues and resource questions.

4. Responsibilities

The job description must also clarify the post-holder's responsibility for the work of others, including their standards, appraisal and development. Is the church administrator responsible for some volunteer workers or the cleaners? Establishing these things clearly gives authority for proper delegation. So this section answers: 'Who is the post-holder supervising?' It is not about the tasks.

5. Primary working relationships

What will the important horizontal relationships be within, and outside, the organisation? This could include other team members. There will also be external people such as suppliers of services, bankers, forums of people with similar jobs, supporters, the media, parallel people in similar organisations, etc. This section is very important. We all need to invest time in relationships with certain key people in order to achieve the best results in the job. So a purchaser needs a good relationship with suppliers, for example, and time invested with them is legitimate. The guide-lines given in this section make clear where relationships are critical to job success, and when endless cups of coffee are not part of the job!

6. Core tasks

These should describe major aspects of the job which continue, year after year. They are the first subdivision after the job title, the first flesh on the bones answering the question,

'What is expected of me?' About ten areas for any one job are normally considered sufficient, as each one will be broken down into subordinate goals. The bulk of these responsibilities will not change. I usually find that if the core tasks are too many or detailed, the job description becomes obsolete very quickly. Another hint: the verbs will give a good indicator about the true seniority if the job title has been too grand.

7. Limits of authority

The job description should spell out what the post-holder can, and cannot, do without reference to someone else. The most common limits are on financial spending, and the hiring and firing of people within the organisation. Other limits might be on overseas travel, printing of promotional material, statements to the media, etc.

8. Key result areas

Many people, including church leaders, have told me that the application of this concept has radically improved their effectiveness. A few claim that it has saved them from a nervous breakdown. For many readers, it will be the most important part of this section. The difficulty with most job descriptions is that they do not take account of changes during tenure. We need some method of moving from 'What is my job?' to 'What does my job mean this year?'

Subtle variations occur over a period of time which most job descriptions do not cater for, so the changes are never documented. This leads to confusion in the expectations. In general, I believe these key result areas should be established by agreement at the annual appraisal, although there is a case for setting some for the unique period of the first six months in the job. We are looking to answer the question, 'If God/my boss is going to say, "Well done thou good and faithful servant," twelve months from now, in what major areas will I have delivered results?' There should be three types of KRAs (Key Result Areas). They should all be similar in importance to the Core tasks.

Group 1. These will be extracted from the Core tasks. They reflect parts of the job that never change, eg a finance director will always have to monitor the budget, a minister will always have to do some preaching. There should be about six such KRAs, summarising the ongoing components of the job.

Group 2. Particular projects this year, eg 'To oversee the completion of the building extension'; 'To see that the accounts are fully computerised'; 'To train up four new home group leaders'. Look for things here that will make big demands on your time in the next twelve months, but not in the following year. These KRAs give seasonal relevance to the job description, and create a dynamic document that lives.

Group 3. Developing people is a core function for leaders. I believe that in any given time span, a leader should always identify two or three names of subordinates to whom they are committing their time. Jesus had twelve such names over a three-year period. Who are you discipling/mentoring/coaching right now? For further details, see Tool 10 on page 173.

Let's summarise the application of this lengthy section. Most people experience difficulty with time management, often with establishing priorities. This is because there is usually no rationale to make them against. We need to have a basis for allocating 'importance'. Key Result Areas give life to a job description and enable decisions about priorities. They interpret the job in a given year. Here is an example of a job description, taken from a missionary society:

JOB TITLE:
Area representative.

JOB PURPOSE:
To promote the work of the mission, to generate practical and spiritual support.

ACCOUNTABILITY:
To the field director.

RESPONSIBILITIES:
Three district representatives

PRIMARY WORKING RELATIONSHIPS:
The other area representatives.
People in similar roles with other missions within my area.

CORE TASKS:
1. To establish new groups of supporters.
2. Conduct 250 meetings per year, raising our profile, fund raising and referring potential new missionaries to the candidates' department.
3. To publicise the work through exhibitions and local media.
4. To recruit and train local volunteer representatives.
5. To maintain full communication with Head Office.
6. To build the Area team.
7. To maintain comprehensive financial records of donations, sales and expenses.
8. To maintain display and video equipment in good repair.
9. To carry out any other reasonable duties as requested by the field director.

LIMITS OF AUTHORITY
To operate within the agreed budget.

KEY RESULT AREAS
1. To generate fresh new work in the schools of Somerset.
2. To undertake a field trip to Kenya producing slide sets for the district representatives.

3. To see that Janet settles into her post in Devon.
4. To recruit 500 new prayer partners.
5. To recruit 100 new donors under thirty years old.
6. To do a mail shot and follow-up phone calls to the Pentecostal churches by May.
7. To spend three days with Fred developing his communication skills.

Writing a single job description is not too difficult, but writing a series of interlocking ones is much harder. Many conflicts arise, and much energy is wasted, out of role confusion. Either two people start the same job without initially realising it, or the task falls between two stools, each leaving it, believing that the other is doing it. No job description will remove this potential. Open and frequent communication is the only solution. The more complex the organisation, the greater the need for internal communication.

How these job descriptions interlock comes from the organisational structure. This determines the lines of accountability and authority. There is no such thing as an innately good or bad structure; often there are quite a few alternatives worth considering. But what should they be measured against? How do we evaluate better and worse structures? The answer is that clear vision is vital to any organisation. Different structures give us varying prospects of fulfilling the vision. This is not principally a book about vision or structures, but I want to point out that in quite a few cases where I have worked as a consultant, the apparent weaknesses in the job descriptions emanated from trying to implement the wrong structures.

VISION
↓
STRUCTURES
↓
JOB DESCRIPTIONS
↓
Goals
↓
Priorities
↓
Plans
↓
Action

Ambiguity

One difficulty in writing effective job descriptions is caused by the increased level of ambiguity that automatically comes with seniority. Most jobs contain technical, administrative and managerial components, but the relative proportions vary with seniority. Higher up the organisation, the technical component diminishes and the managerial percentage increases. At a junior level, it is possible to prescribe duties, but as we move up the ladder, there are more areas of responsibility and it is not possible to define these so precisely.

A horizontal cross-section near the top of the diagram contains more management than technical components, compared with the opposite near the bottom of the diagram. For the sake of clarity, I've left the administrative elements as constant, although they might vary as we move up the diagram.

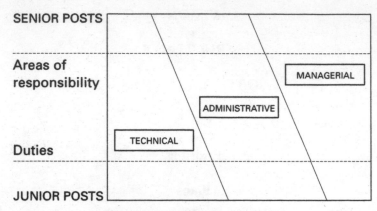

Figure 14. Living with ambiguity

The model shows us the difficulty in writing senior job descriptions. For example, a junior financial assistant might have duties like:

To accurately record petty cash transactions.
To acknowledge all donations, with thanks, by the end of the following working day.
To file all letters in your department within one week of writing them.

A senior post might include things like:

To prepare and monitor the budget.
To present comprehensible summaries of the financial situation to board members.

Some new managers don't find the transition to living with greater ambiguity at all easy. If they have been offered senior posts largely out of high technical skills, then the transition can be particularly painful. The summary message is simple: the more senior the position, the more we need to live with ambiguity.

Action

1. If you have not got job descriptions for yourself and other leaders, produce them in the format I have used above.
2. Establish KRAs for each of these people for the next six months and discuss them together.
3. Look for potential overlap and tasks which are escaping everybody.

References

Cormack, David, *Seconds Away!* (MARC Europe: England, 1986).

Timpe, A. Dale, editor, *The Management of Time* (Facts on File Publications: Oxford, 1987).

Pearson, Barrie, *Common Sense Time Management for Personal Success* (Mercury Business Books: London, 1988).

Hocheister, Robert M., *Time Management* (Cassell, Business Success Guides: London, 1995).

TOOL 4

DELEGATION

I would suggest that delegation is the single most important leadership skill, partly because it creates the time for you to do the rest of your job. Most time management books rightly have a section on delegation, but there are very few books totally devoted to the subject. Even then, the emphasis is virtually exclusively on the principal reason for delegation, producing results and benefits for the delegator. The majority of delegations are done for this reason, but the opportunity for people development, the second reason, also interests us. Delegation is one of the easier tools to apply from this book and the impact on people development can be quite dramatic.

There is a clear mental blockage that I have experienced from clients attending training courses; people will only learn if they want to! The old joke was, 'How many counsellors does it take to change a light bulb?' 'Six, but only provided that the light bulb really wants to change!' It is very similar with delegation. Using the tool effectively requires both the right attitudes and a high skill level in the delegator. If the attitudes aren't appropriate, then the skills won't be acquired. Therefore we need to look separately at attitudes and skills.

The right attitudes

1. Personal security

We are all somewhere on a continuum between being totally secure and being completely insecure. It's no help to tell me that I am insecure unless you can identify something about the manifestations, the sources and the remedies. Insecure people don't delegate readily, but I think that statement is too general to tell us the real story. The specific insecurity is the fear of doing yourself out of a job. We would often hear leaders say that they want to make themselves redundant, but it is much more challenging when it actually starts to happen. I've done it once, and with hindsight, it was the making of another leader. At the time it was highly disconcerting! If you personally are well managed by your superiors, there truly isn't a danger. If you are concerned about the views of other people, the importance of your ability to nurture your team will be recognised and, as we have said, you will also have more time for other important tasks.

2. Risk taking

Any delegation that involves the potential for development also involves the possibility of an imperfect outcome. There is an additional risk that is less obvious and longer term; if we don't involve people, then they will drift away of their own accord. The secret lies in assessing and managing the risk, not trying to remove the possibility altogether, and we will discuss how this can be done later in the chapter. If there has never been a possibility of a subordinate doing an imperfect job or making a mistake, then you have never made an important delegation.

3. Trust

When I ask folk at seminars about the principal attitudes needed for good delegation, frequently the first answer is 'trust'. Then I ask, 'What does trust mean?' Usually it means that the delegatee will do a good job. This couldn't be further from the truth. Trust should be independent of results. Trust is the quality of the bridge between us that remains even after a serious shortfall in results. It may mean that we expect people to give things their best shot, and that communication channels will be open if the delegatee is experiencing difficulties. In turn, they may have expectations about support and honest feedback. The first recorded delegation, which was from God to man, was made knowing that Adam would fail (Genesis 1:26).

4. Commitment to the growth of others

Perhaps this is the single most constructive attitude needed for effective delegation. From the outset, the good leader is not trying to produce dependency or followership. There needs to be the hope and belief that others will achieve more than we ever have or will. 'He will do even greater things than these' (John 14:12) says Jesus. It's quite logical to say that about areas where we are not strong, but it is harder to want this when the issues touch our strengths. This is actually the more frequent difficulty, since we often attract people with similar gifts.

5. Being prepared to give commensurate authority

Many delegations fail because delegators like to give jobs without letting go of clout. It is not enough to give away tasks; we need to give the authority that is necessary to complete them, and we may need to communicate explicitly that this authority has been given. My understanding of the Greek *apostollos* is that it contains the concept of 'in my name'. For this biblical role, it was as though Jesus were there. They were acting on his behalf. The leader must give away authority just as generously, which will include the freedom to make mistakes. In my consultancy role, I have found that more delegations go wrong because of mistakes made by the delegator rather than by the delegatee. Failing to relinquish authority is the most frequent error.

6. Holding people to account

With authority comes accountability. You should not hold somebody accountable if you haven't given them authority. If you are not prepared to tolerate risks and failures you may well prefer programmed robots to people. The only method of accomplishing certain tasks, letting go of a measure of authority, will have additional risks. Let's also note at this stage that accountability is the learning tool, not a punishing stick; there is no learning without accountability.

7. Accepting responsibility

We have acquired this dreadful expression 'the buck stops here'. Where does it stop and where should it stop? I sometimes think that if a nurse breaks a cup in a hospital this afternoon, the opposition party would like the Secretary of State for Health to resign immediately! There are times when the authority has been passed a long way down the line and the buck stops with a junior person. Ministers (of State!) are often reluctant to accept responsibility, but they cannot be held responsible for every incident. The key message is that the buck stops where the authority is. If we never let go of authority then the buck would permanently stop with us. The implication then is that one person in an organisation is ultimately accountable for everything. That is too big a burden to carry, but it is also, too often, a device for clinging on to power.

The right skills

If our attitudes are right, we can now go on to acquire the skills. I am repeatedly amazed how reluctant some leaders are when faced with a steep learning curve in their delegation skills. They retreat to trying to do everything themselves, rather than looking for the lessons in the situations that go wrong. Good delegators are not born; just as in sport, practice does not make perfect, but it makes practice easier!

There are two principal skills in delegation, each with many aspects:

1. Matching people and tasks

This is a very important skill. Remember that we cannot motivate anybody; motivation comes from within. The benefits of the pep talk are very short lived, and the only long-term method of motivating members is to match square pegs with square holes, etc. By giving the bigger picture, showing how the task fits into a greater plan, we can gain substantial commitment for a short period. But on a long-term basis, either the task excites an individual or it doesn't. The implications are formidable. Leaders need to spend considerable time looking at the strengths and weaknesses of the people they manage, and need to understand what is involved in various tasks around them in order to match people and tasks. It is not necessary for the leader to have done all the tasks, but they need to have a clear idea of the skills required and the approximate time-scale for completion.

It is often said, 'Don't appoint an overqualified person.' If there is no challenge for them, they are likely to move on quite quickly and we are left with the additional costs of further interviewing. Well, the same is true of delegation. If the task contains little challenge, then the needs of certain individuals (those high in achievement motivation) will not be met. When they are bored, they start saying, 'I can do that with my eyes closed!' and all but literally do. Then they make careless mistakes and we undervalue their skills still further. It is the delegator's fault for de-skilling them.

2. Communication

Good communication is the very life-blood of delegation. It underpins every stage of the process. The time spent communicating could be seen as wasted, but in reality is an investment that repays many times over.

At the outset, the task must be clearly described. Usually too much emphasis is placed on how to do the job, without enough detail on the standard of the end product. State clearly what is to be achieved, agree on a convenient deadline, but don't focus too much on how to do it. The style summarised by 'I'll get it up and running and then hand it over to you' is particularly unhelpful. The best way for somebody else to do the task may not be the way that I did it. The purpose, goal and standard are paramount, not the process and method. At the end of the initial conversation, the delegatee must go away with the same mental snapshot of the completed situation as the delegator came with.

During the process, quality communication must continue. A review is not a post-mortem. It must be possible to ask how things are going before a disaster is unavoidable. If there are unforeseen difficulties, let's have a chat. Interim deadlines must be monitored. Extra resources may be needed. How this monitoring stage is viewed depends largely on trust. Too often the delegator calls it 'just keeping tabs on things', but the delegatee sees it as 'breathing down my neck'. Trust is so critical here. As we shall see later, it's not just the words that matter, but the meaning put on these words. Whether we like it or not, it's the receiver of the words who ascribes the meaning. So it is vital that the delegator is satisfied that the delegatee really does understand the briefing.

Finally, to enable learning and for accountability to be meaningful, there needs to be a debriefing session afterwards. This could be about the lessons that might be learnt, or just a great opportunity to give some praise and say thanks.

Don't be put off by these skills. There are only two of them, but they deserve constant attention. We can always improve, and any improvements will yield a rich dividend. But it's easier to work on these things once they have been articulated.

Degrees of delegation

Part of the confusion that occurs during communication is that at different times we may mean different things by 'delegation'. There is really a sliding scale, but I'll describe some points on the scale for convenience. The variable is the degree of authority released by the delegator.

1. Please do the initial research. I'll decide.
2. Give me the strengths and weaknesses of the options. I'll decide.
3. Recommend actions for my approval.
4. Let me know what you want to do. Wait for my approval.
5. Let me know what you want to do. Do it, unless I say otherwise.
6. Take action. Please keep me informed.
7. Take action. Bring any problems to me and we'll discuss them.
8. Take action. No feedback is necessary; it's entirely in your court.

Frequently and unfortunately there are two others, but I'm not sure they deserve placing on the scale!

1. 'Do it, do it the way I showed you, and do it by yesterday!'

Sometimes this is necessary, either with a particularly difficult member of staff, or in an emergency. The fewer things categorised as emergencies the better, because there is no opportunity for developing people when there are tight deadlines.

   2. 'I'm not sure how to do this, boss!'
     'OK, leave it with me.'

This is called upward delegation, a skilful science used by busy subordinates. For whatever reason, they ask enough questions so that their superior takes the job back. The story goes about a junior rushing into the boss's office. 'Boy, have we got a problem,' he says. The boss retorted, 'Boy, you have!'

Reasons why we fail to delegate

It might be worth considering the reasons for not delegating; they are quite personal to different delegators. We know delegation makes sense, so let's think about what is stopping us. Some of the following suggestions contain more than a grain of truth. For example, you might be able to do the job better or more quickly, but that doesn't mean that you should be doing it. Tick any of these reasons that you feel are particularly applicable to you (see figure 15 on page 106).

   Here is a summary of the key points so far, and a few extra hints, in tabular form (see figure 16 on page 107).

Delegation for development

I have deliberately left the major implications until the end of the section. What impact should delegation skills have on our ability to develop leaders?

   It seems to me that there are essentially two types of delegation; let's call them type A and type B for now. Usually, delegation involves creating a list of jobs and finding people to do them, which I am calling type A. But it

BLOCKS TO DELEGATION

1. I don't want them to think that I'm lazy.
2. I cannot afford mistakes in this type of work.
3. Their skill levels are not high enough.
4. There isn't time to delegate; I can do it quicker myself.
5. They might let me down.
6. I enjoy doing this myself.
7. They are already too busy.
8. I like to lead by example.
9. It's my job.
10. I'd like the credit for doing a proper job.
11. They might do it better!
12. Poor selection of the appropriate person in the past.
13. My inability to balance workloads.
14. My delegation skills are weak.
15. I assume that the most competent person is the right person.
16. I delegate writing any other personal reasons to you!

Figure 15

is possible to run the process the other way round. From an appraisal interview or even an informal chat, we could identify experiences and opportunities from which a member might benefit. We could agree challenging possibilities for them to cut their teeth on (type B).

Both these types of delegation are legitimate. Type B delegations are exciting and quite different in nature. They are less frequent; it would be unrealistic to assume that most delegations can be challenging and tailor made to the person. Many delegations (all the type A situations) are routine and mundane. But if one in ten delegations is specifically designed for the delegatee, the whole atmosphere

	DO	DON'T
1.	Plan	React
2.	Spend lots of time thinking about matching people and jobs	Grab the nearest available person
3.	Emphasise the end product and standards	Give too much detail about 'how'
4.	Give self-contained jobs to individuals	Ask lots of people to do it, in the hope that somebody might
5.	Agree clear deadlines	Say, 'As soon as possible'
6.	Communicate fully	Jib at the time spent in communication
7.	Give commensurate authority	Give jobs without authority
8.	Expect questions and dialogue	Talk too much yourself
9.	Show how the task integrates into the bigger picture	Give isolated, unconnected tasks without details about the context
10.	Review progress regularly	Wait for a post-mortem, or breathe down necks
11.	Be available	Take the job back
12.	Go direct to the person for an update	Ask others how the job is progressing
13.	Give credit for the successes	Want the glory
14.	Take the rap	Dump the blame
15.	DELEGATE	ABDICATE

Figure 16

changes and you will get a more positive response on the donkey work. If ten out of ten are mundane, then folk will feel put upon. Obviously, there is more risk involved in these developmental delegations, so we need to be more available and generally improve the communication. Some of the defining features of the two types are:

Type A	Type B
Focus on the results	Focus on the development of the person
Frequent	Rare
Lower risks	Higher risks
Requiring less supervision	Requiring more supervision
Requiring less availability	Requiring more availability
Needs less informal time	Needs more informal time
There is a routine	Usually a one-off task
Clear instructions	Better two-way dialogue

Figure 17

As I said at the beginning of the chapter, the wider use of delegation for developmental purposes may well prove to be one of the easier tools to use from this book, but it might involve a significant change of emphasis for you. It takes the leaders to talk to members and find out their hopes and to identify where they see the potential opportunities. We'll look at the right type of questions to generate this sort of discussion in Tool 9.

Action

Agree an hour in your diary to spend with each of your key subordinates. The meeting deserves advance thinking time towards an agreed agenda. The issues should be:

'Where do you want to be five years from now?'
'What opportunities and experiences do you need to get there?'
'How can we help you realise those hopes?'
'Which bit of my job would you like to cut your teeth on?'
'Which elements of the work have you never tried, but which excite you?'
'What could I immediately delegate to you which you would enjoy?'

References

Jenks, James M. and Kelly, John M., *Don't Do, Delegate* (Kogan Page: London, 1986).
Schwarz, Andrew, *Delegating Authority* (Cassell, Business Success Guides: London, 1995).

GAINING FROM SUCCESS AND FAILURE

In his poem, 'If', Rudyard Kipling describes triumph and disaster as 'these twin imposters.' For too many people, a decade is one year of such experiences, repeated ten times over. As leaders we have a particular responsibility to learn from experiences and to model learning from them. Constructively learning from the past is a vital opportunity for leadership development. Start by thinking of a specific goal or task which you failed to reach in the last three years. Please be as honest with yourself as possible.

1. Write down the major cause of the failure to achieve the task that you are considering. The major cause of my failure was:

_____

_____

_____

2. In number 1, have you described a cause which is due to something about you (eg 'I didn't work hard enough') or something due to other people and circumstances (eg 'not enough support from the team')? Mark your assessment on this ten-point scale.

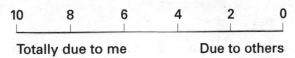

3. Consider the cause which you described in number 1. Is it likely to recur in the future? (eg 'I always underestimate the amount of work involved' or 'The congregation is never as supportive as I hope'.) Or, will the cause never recur? (Eg 'I've learnt my lesson' or 'It was a unique combination of circumstances and people'.) Mark the assessment on the scale.

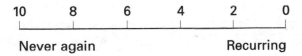

4. Did the cause affect just one of your activities or did it have a wider effect on a range of activities? Mark your score on the scale.

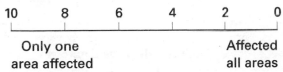

5. Considering the failure in retrospect, what has been the long-term impact? Mark your assessment on the scale.

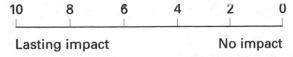

6. Was the failure that you selected typical of the sort of failures that you experience? Mark your score on the scale.

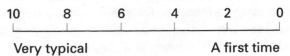

Failing and failure

One swallow does not make a summer, it just makes one swallow! Equally, one failing (a mistake or a trait) does not make a failure (a person). We should differentiate between the sin and the sinner, the act and the actor, the failing and the person who has failed. This is not only Christian and biblical, but also essential if we are going to deal positively with failings. I'm suggesting that this is just as important in enhancing leadership as in a general counselling situation. Feeling a failure is very destructive, which makes our responsibility to learn from mistakes all the greater. The first stage in learning from a failure is being prepared to label it for what it is. If we deny its nature, we won't learn from it. Being able to separate the incident and the person also gives us much higher prospects of improving. People who have learned to view failure through God's eyes frequently emerge with a deeper and gentler character.

Cause and effect

In this section we will particularly deal with results and reactions which are illustrated in the cycle below. Thoughts determine what we feel and think, repeated thought processes determine our motivation, and our motivation is the main spring of our actions. So our attitude to successes and failures determines how we approach future situations.

Results and reactions

As goals are measurable and have a time limit, ultimately there can only be two possible outcomes – success or failure. Our reaction to successes or failures can either be positive or negative. I can feel bad about achieving a goal, for example if I realise that a much higher goal could have been set and

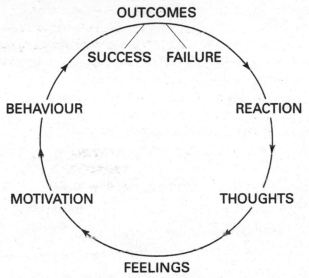

Figure 18. The attribution cycle

achieved. It's also possible to feel good about a failure, perhaps by realising that what I have learnt is of greater benefit in the long term, or by accepting that I reached a very good result purely because I set such a demanding goal. For example, if I set out to share my faith with twenty people this year, and actually reach nineteen, that might still be a 'good' result but a 'failure' against my set goal. I have also known people who love being counselled to be very pleased with failure; it gets them more time from the counsellor! We attribute our successes and failures to causes. The nature of those causes determines our reaction to the results.

Attribution

Whether we experience patterns of success or failure is determined by our understanding of the cause. There are very practical applications of attribution, especially when helping

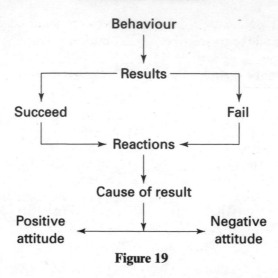

Figure 19

the 'failure' to regain control of their cause and effect cycle. I suspect that we can learn more from failures and hence I am focusing on failure, but the tool applies equally to a success outcome. Think back to your own maths lessons at school (if you can bear to!). A page full of ticks after your homework was returned gave a brief warm glow. The red cross was different. Questions that you were getting wrong, and continued to get wrong, certainly achieved nothing. It's the questions that you were getting wrong and later could do properly, where the improvement and satisfaction lay.

There are three main dimensions of attribution:

1. Focus dimension. Internal or external causes.
2. Dynamic dimension. Static or unstable causes.
3. Control dimension. Controllable or uncontrollable causes.

The focus dimension

This dimension causes us to place the reasons for success or failure within ourselves (internal) or outside ourselves (external). Here are some examples of causes of success and failure and the corresponding attribution:

Internal causes	External causes
Ability	Chance
Effort	Support
Strategy	Environment
Motivation	Timing
Experience	Leadership/Membership 'Them'
Personality	God (could be internal)

Figure 20. The focus dimension

Go back to the exercise at the beginning of the section. Your answer to number 2 should tell you whether you saw the reason as internal or external. It's not always easy to decide. For example, 'I was aiming to make lots of money' is obviously an internal statement. 'Legal work is a well-paid field' is superficially external, but contains an underlying sentiment that 'I went into it for that reason'; hence the source is more debatable.

There is a link between focus and self-esteem. When successes are attributed to internal causes, self-esteem is likely to grow. Conversely, if failures are attributed to internal factors, self-esteem will fall. The external focus does not influence self-esteem to the same extent, eg 'It wasn't really my fault, the weather was awful.' But neither is there the opportunity for the successes to bolster us: 'If I hadn't happened to bump into the boss, we might never have managed to do it.' Such statements don't offer much to feed on! We can summarise the possible impact of success and failure on self-esteem in this way (see figure 21 on page 116).

Individuals who have a tendency to attribute successes to box 2 and failures to box 3, that is they blame themselves for

	Internal focus	External focus
Success	1. Positive self-esteem	2. Little impact on self-esteem
Failure	3. Negative self-esteem	4. Protection of self-esteem

Figure 21

failure and attribute the cause of successes to others, often suffer from feelings of pessimism and loss of control. An orientation towards boxes 1 and 4 results in a more robust self-image and a more positive view of the future. In church-based work, I find many people unable to feed off success. If it goes wrong, then it's their fault, but if it goes well, then to God be the glory. It's important to take satisfaction from successes.

Effort and ability

Within the internal factors on the focus dimension, one pair has a significant and frequent influence on our behaviour. This is the effort/ability pairing. When results are attributed to *effort*, the danger is an increased anxiety, reducing the prospects of future success: 'We only just made it and we were working flat out.' However, when high efforts result in failure, then we tend to feel shame and humiliation since, despite our efforts, we failed, and therefore our failure must be reattributed to our lack of *ability*.

Ability is much more important to self-esteem than effort. We can choose how much effort we put in, but we think that we have much less choice over our ability levels. This can lead to a very real danger. If we might fail despite high effort, then in order to protect our self-esteem (which is based on ability), it's safer to put in low effort. This is a mental coping

strategy anticipating the possibility of failure. So, to pre-serve a self-concept of high ability, we prefer to deduce that:
High ability plus high effort gives us our successes.
High ability plus low effort gives us our failures.

Therefore, if failure seems likely, we will protect our self-esteem by minimising effort, and of course in doing so we increase the risk of failure. Many children have failed examinations through this attitude, especially when faced with excessive expectations from others. It's better not to try, and then they have got an excuse when they fail.

The dynamic dimension

We may see causes as internal, but also fixed. If we attribute our failures to static causes, then we do not expect situations to improve. There is nothing to be done: we must just learn to live with it. In acute situations, this can lead to a deep sense of helplessness. This is bred by putting early failures down to internal, stable factors. Further examples can then be made to reinforce the rationale: 'It's hopeless, I'll never be able to. . .' or 'What's the use, I'll never change.' On the other hand, the good thing about attributing success to static causes is that there will be a rise in personal expectations. Having been successful once, and for a stable reason, we can anticipate positive outcomes again.

Instability in the cause sadly results in less confidence when we succeed, but more hope when we fail. On balance, it is much better to regard the cause as unstable. Your answer to number 3 will tell you how you saw this feature in your chosen example. Here are some examples with the appropriate allocation on this second dimension (see figure 22 on page 118).

STATIC CAUSES	UNSTABLE CAUSES
Ability	Effort
Personality	Motivation
Culture	Climate
Appearance	Timing
Character	Chance

Figure 22. The dynamic dimension

The clue to recognising these attitudes is the use of the words 'always' and 'never'. Both are symptomatic of static causes.

The helpless (failure due to static causes) and the depressed (failure due to internal causes) are characterised by:

Taking less responsibility for outcomes.
Attributing failure to the lack of ability.
Seeing themselves as having less influence over outcomes.
Viewing adverse circumstances as being insurmountable.
Tending not to respond to failure with either increased effort or persistence ('What's the use?').

The control dimension

Were the causes deemed to be within our control? For example, the amount of effort that we put into preparing a sermon. Or were they outside our control? For example, the flu epidemic that caused us to lose the vote at the Annual General Meeting. If we attribute failure to factors outside our control, our expectation of success will be low with the likelihood that less effort will be put in. Then there will be performance difficulties which could be controlled but are not. If the causes of failure are seen as outside our control but within the control of others, then anger and resentment can arise. Later evidence will be in low motivation, depression and deterioration in health.

Good management of conflict often breaks down in this way. Either we see anger as external ('You made me. . .') or internal. Anger is a choice despite the size of the provocation. We need the right attributional approach to bring the issue within our own control. Anger should always be attributed to internal, controllable causes.

Handling failure maturely

Failure can be managed, indeed it can be used constructively, if we analyse our thought patterns and change our attributional styles. The failure is still there, but we can regain control and take responsibility for our own lives and learning. The mature position is to view the usual causes of failure as:

Predominantly INTERNAL	ie I am responsible.
Partly UNSTABLE	ie Nothing is fixed.
Open to CONTROL	ie I can do something.

Action to help us deal with failure

1. Regard ability as 'unstable' ie variable. Nobody knows or has reached their full potential.
2. Attribute the failure to effort rather than ability.
3. Attribute failure to a deficient strategy which can be improved.
4. Avoid setting goals that are designed to demonstrate ability.
5. Avoid competitive situations in which we aggressively pursue our own goals at the expense of other people's goals.
6. Avoid perfectionism, but aim for improvement and excellence.
7. See failure as an opportunity. Monitor performance and try to learn something from every failure.

8. Take responsibility for our goals.
9. Give goals a task focus, eg 'I want to do' not 'I want to be'.
10. Avoid defending self-esteem. We can't. We are worth-ful and that's fixed, eternal and from the highest authority.

There are some big messages for leaders here as you help others to grow. Particularly, it's important to get the timing right in helping people to face failure. I've seen this handled badly in Christian situations. I find many ministers who move during their work from one church to the next one without learning from their mistakes. When they leave, their emotional reservoirs are low and they don't want to face the questions. After a period of recovery, when things are going better during the 'honeymoon' period, they see little point in raking over old ground, so the issues remain unresolved. The honeymoon period is a great time for burying uncomfortable issues. Similarly congregations don't change, and wait in ambush for the next incumbent. I've known many missionaries come home on furlough with the same mentality. The only way to break into this cycle is to face the failure, with good support structures, but while the questions still seem real and fresh.

There are similarities between this Tool and Tool 8. Both involve changing our mental tapes which can become so familiar that we assume that they are fixed. I'm not advocating an extreme stance, often thought of as 'the power of positive thinking'. But I am saying that there needs to be mental self-discipline so that we can constructively change the way we think, and eliminate the bad mental practices which lead to unnecessary stress and a grave loss of effectiveness.

Action

Now review your answers to the exercise at the beginning of this chapter. What have you learnt about your mental tapes that will help you in the future?

USING DIFFERENT LEARNING STYLES

I'd like you to have a go at this exercise 'cold', without an introduction. I'll explain the implications fully later. There are no right or wrong answers. Try to be as honest as you can; no outcomes are better than others.

Score each of the following questions:

2 points if you strongly agree
1 point if you agree more than you disagree
0 points if you disagree.

1. I relish the tension and pressure of crises. ____
2. In my written work I am something of a perfectionist, making lots of minor modifications before being satisfied with the finished product. ____
3. I find ambiguity quite uncomfortable; I like to know where I stand. ____
4. Theory is only important when we can apply it to everyday life. ____
5. I am more interested in specifically factual discussions than social chat. ____
6. I write concise memos summarising the key points. ____

7. During discussions I can usually support my case with clear reasoning.   ____

8. I am easily bored by repetitive work.   ____

9. In discussion, I am known for the sensible, feasible contributions.   ____

10. I have scant regard for protocol and the established way of doing things.   ____

11. Generally, I think that slow decisions based on careful thought are usually more accurate than those based on gut feelings.   ____

12. I regard myself as a very divergent thinker, and usually have lots of fresh ideas.   ____

13. I am regarded as clear thinking and unemotional in my decision making.   ____

14. I enjoy thinking about a range of scenarios and usually have a fall-back position.   ____

15. Clear understanding of the complete picture is very important to me.   ____

16. In meetings I am conscious of the politics that lie behind the superficial comments.   ____

17. I see myself as a transparent character; what you see is what you get.   ____

18. I am part of a wide network with whom I chat about up-to-date technical information in my field.   ____

19. The 'best way' of doing something is determined by cost and speed.   ____

20. I believe that variety and novelty are more important than practicality and efficiency.   ____

21. I shy away from role play or other situations where I may not have all the information.   ____

22. I am often the person who turns plans into action.   ____

23. I seldom consider all the possible consequences of my actions. _____

24. I take an orderly approach when I face new situations. _____

25. I think that complex data deserves careful scrutiny; the headlines are not enough. _____

26. I like improving suggestions that others put forward. _____

27. I believe that if a job is worth doing, then it's worth doing properly. _____

28. I believe that good meetings are short and discussions should keep to the point. _____

29. I can easily put the mistakes of the past behind me and focus on the present opportunities. _____

30. I hold clear and strong beliefs on many issues. _____

31. I don't like cutting corners to meet schedules set by others. _____

32. I am structured and organised both in my actions and thinking. _____

33. I actively look for challenges in the form of new opportunities and experiences. _____

34. I like to glean comments from a wide spectrum of people before offering my own alternatives or comments. _____

35. I believe that the end is more important than the means. _____

36. I ask people about their motives and rationale rather than accepting their statements at face value. _____

37. Taken by and large, I prefer talking to listening. _____

38. I believe that too often formal procedures are a hindrance, rather than proving to be beneficial. _____

39. Delivering a good job, on time, is more important than taking account of people's feelings.   ____

40. I listen carefully to other people's contributions before offering my own opinion.   ____

41. I tend to see trends and patterns rather than a series of isolated, unconnected events.   ____

42. Background detail is not important; what matters is 'Does it work?'   ____

43. I find it easier to work with methodical, analytical people rather than those with an intuitive approach.   ____

44. I am known for being blunt, direct and straightforward.   ____

45. It is better to make measured responses rather than to be spontaneous.   ____

46. I can usually spot the flaws and holes in other people's proposals.   ____

47. I find that spontaneous actions based on feelings often prove as accurate as those derived from detailed planning and analysis.   ____

48. I like to consider all the alternatives before making up my mind.   ____

Score sheet

Please enter your scores next to the appropriate question numbers using the score sheet on page 131. (Note that they are not in the usual numerical order!)

Different people learn best in different ways, and in order to develop leadership it is important to understand which type of learning opportunity is most appropriate for a particular individual.

There are four basic approaches to learning:

Activists

Activists will have a go at anything and there's no time like the present. There is very little cynicism and they will try new ideas without bias or prejudice. Stickability is not their strong point because variety is the spice of life. New things are exciting and are usually better just for being new. They are exuberant, but sometimes appear self-centred, because the hands-on experience is all consuming. Detail is unimportant; they don't mind making fools of themselves. Essentially they have a short-term attitude: eat, drink and be merry for tomorrow we can do the same again! Planning should be left out of the dictionary.

In the early days of computing, if you gave a machine to an activist, they would immediately attach the plug, switch on and start typing. Soon they were likely to lose a few pages of text, but that's much better than reading the manual. Sometimes we ask course delegates how they learned to drive a car, and the highest ever activist scorer said, 'I stole one and finally left it parked in a shop window.' At his second attempt, he reversed into a bollard as he tried to master the gear lever!

We went on holiday one year with a couple of close friends; his activist score is very high. After a long and (to me) tiring journey, he leapt to his feet on the first evening and said, 'Right, what are we going to do together tonight?' The reflector of the group replied, 'What do you mean by "we" and "do"?' The activist has high energy levels. I suspect that our historical approach to higher education has failed to serve activists well. Lectures and seminars leave them quickly bored. As we will see in the next section, their expectations of feedback will also be very different from the more detached standpoint.

Activists learn best from:

Short duration activities
A personally high profile in the situation
The opportunity for quick decisions
Opportunities where the consequences of mistakes are not severe.

Which of your team are activists?

Reflectors

For any feature you can imagine about activists, then just about the opposite will be true of reflectors. No decision should be rushed. If you ask them how they are feeling, they would probably prefer to think about it and tell you tomorrow. They like to watch how things are done, and come to conclusions with great reluctance. You never know, there might be some new information coming along soon. Reflectors listen carefully, weigh up the pros and cons, analyse data against previous experiences, but hold strongly to the positions that they finally take. In meetings they are reluctant to make their contributions, and definitely won't be drawn at an early stage. When they do come to a conclusion, they will commit themselves very deeply to the outcome. They are not the pioneers in change, but once the benefits are clear, they will not be deflected from the path lightly.

In learning to drive a car, they will watch from the back seat for some time, ask lots of questions, and eventually will want to be really proficient rather than just learn the minimum needed to pass the test. When first faced with a computer, they will ask others to show them how to use the machine, be reluctant to commit themselves to the keyboard, and will read the manual carefully.

Reflectors learn best when they:

Have time to think
Can learn from their mistakes
Are not exposed, especially to ridicule
Have all the possible information.

Theorists

For the theorists, all observations and data must fit into little boxes. Nothing happens in isolation. They are interested in models, logic, blueprints, rationale and values. If a job is worth doing well, then they should know why and how it works. Theorists are often perfectionists who like all the small print and are not just content with the broad swathes. Good decisions are reached by orderly approaches, one step at a time. They don't like ambiguity, and unusual, contrary data is very uncomfortable. Paradigms are constructed and strongly adhered to, sometimes too rigidly.

Their approach to driving lessons might be: if you don't know the firing cycle of the four cylinders in a car, then you shouldn't be driving it. For computer learning, everybody should know the terminology – bits and bytes not bits and bobs. Their philosophy is 'Let's take the back off and find out why it works.' Rather like the reflectors, they will be reluctant to jump in, but instead of just needing more time, they are likely to want a more comprehensive explanation.

Theorists learn best from:

Purposeful activities
Situations where the underlying assumptions can be
   questioned

Opportunities where there are mental links with other
situations and they can make connections
The complexity of the situation is stimulating.

Pragmatists

Pragmatists are real life practical people who see the acid test
as 'Does it work?' and 'Can it be made to work better?' Just
as the activists, they like experience more than thinking.
They can be impatient with thinkers and are excited about
the potential of new possibilities. They respond positively to
challenges as long as the results are within their own control.
Faced with a new software package, they ask, 'What are the
advantages compared with the current system?' Having seen
the benefits, they would introduce applications throughout
the organisation, with little thought to ideas like gaining
people commitment in the management of change. If car
driving is more convenient than the train, how quickly can I
get through my test?

Pragmatists learn best when:

The situations are real rather than hypothetical
There will be efficiency savings
Teamwork and relationships do not threaten
    expediency
The outcome is more important than the process.

There is no such thing as a better or worse profile across
these learning styles. Essentially we need a balance across the
styles to maximise the opportunities presented to us. If you
have a particularly low score in any style, it can be a real
handicap. Here are some of the potential dangers of one
particularly low score:

Low activists   Reluctant to experiment
                      Concerned about failure
                      Too much thinking.

Low reflectors	Make mistakes but don't learn from them
	Miss possible improvements that require thinking time
	Neglect potential consequences.
Low theorists	Miss patterns to experiences and mistakes
	Miss the greater conviction which can be gained from a mental framework
	Tend to be unable to win others to their viewpoint.
Low pragmatists	Miss opportunities through being too theoretical
	Focus on justification and persuasion
	Find that improvements take too long.

In developing leadership, we must remember that the fastest growth comes from matching the learning style to the individual. The same experience may benefit a variety of people, but remember that activists will want to be 'hands on' quickly, reflectors need time and space, theorists need the fullest explanations and pragmatists apply the 'expediency test'.

However, we can learn from the scientific model of:

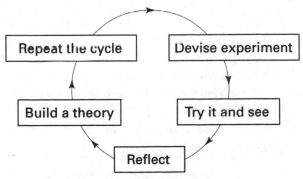

Figure 23. The learning cycle

which relies on bringing all the styles to bear in the right order. By choosing to improve our attitude to opportunities with which we are less comfortable, we can become more rounded and balanced in our approach, actually resulting in better and more complete learning and retention. By playing mainly to your stronger styles, your learning will lack reinforcement and therefore be much slower. Although people are fairly set in their ways, this is not a psychometric test, ie the results are not necessarily fixed. We can raise our skill levels in unfamiliar styles.

As with previous tools, there are therefore two levels of applying the insights of this section. If you are trying to develop someone

Who is still relatively insecure
Who is a low risk taker
Who has not grown dramatically recently.

then it is necessary to start providing opportunities in the style that is most accessible and comfortable. If you are helping a more mature, positive person who is on a high growth curve at the time, then encourage them to experiment with styles outside their first preference.

Action

1. How did you learn to drive a car or use a computer? Did you enjoy the experience?
2. Take some time to think back over some seasons of your life when you have experienced real growth and a steep learning curve. Did the methods of learning substantiate the results of this test?
3. Take your colleagues through the exercise and discuss their results with them.

ACTIVIST	REFLECTOR	THEORIST	PRAGMATIST
1	2	3	4
8	5	7	6
10	11	13	9
12	16	15	14
17	18	21	19
20	25	24	22
23	27	30	26
29	31	32	28
33	34	36	35
37	40	41	39
38	45	43	42
47	48	46	44
Total:	Total:	Total:	Total:

Norms

Please circle your band for each of the four learning styles to illustrate your preferences and profile.

	ACTIVIST	REFLECTOR	THEORIST	PRAGMATIST
Very high	15–24	19–24	20–24	16–24
High	12–14	16–18	17–19	13–15
Medium	10–11	14–15	15–16	11–12
Low	7–9	10–13	11–14	8–10
Very low	0–6	0–9	0–10	0–7

Reference

Kolb, David B., *Experiential Learning: Experience as the Source of Learning and Development* (Prentice-Hall: Englewood Cliffs, NJ, 1984).

TOOL 7

APPRAISALS, SUPERVISION AND FEEDBACK

We have looked at attribution, a tool for helping us to learn from our mistakes. But sometimes our learning is rather muted; we need feedback from others in order to see things clearly. We are not always capable of reflecting accurately on our own actions. I think part of the reason is that looking back and assigning negative comments to previous events smacks of judgementalism. 'Do not judge, or you too will be judged' (Matthew 7:1) and, should you need any more evidence, 'No-one who puts his hand to the plough and looks back is fit for service in the kingdom of God' (Luke 9:62). But ploughmen having their lunch like to look back over the fields that they ploughed in the morning. It's encouraging! Sometimes we need the insights of others if we are to maximise our growth from the opportunity of reviewing.

The concept of reviewing and learning is as old as Genesis. The secret lies in why we do it, and the reason should always be so that we can improve. Six times in the creation account God looked and saw that it was good, once it was very good, and once it wasn't good (for man to live alone).

The practice of reviewing is consistent throughout Scripture:

'She did what she could' (Mark 14:8).
'This is my Son, whom I love; with him I am well pleased'
    (Matthew 3:17).
'It is finished' (John 19:30).
'Well done, good and faithful servant' (Matthew 25:21).

In the letters to the seven churches (Revelation 2 and 3) there
is a common pattern. All of them contain the phrase 'I know
your works'. All of them contain messages of performance-
based encouragement, all contain criticism and all contain
methods of improving in the future.

I firmly believe that everybody wants to grow, mature and
develop. If I join a church or organisation, I want the sure
knowledge that if I was leaving in five years' time, then I
would have grown in character, knowledge and skill.
Initially, it is fine to tell me, 'Just get your feet under the table;
we can do some of this growing business later.' But if I don't
see others growing within the organisation, and things don't
begin to move on for me later, then eventually disappoint-
ment and dissatisfaction will take over. In summary, all
employees and volunteers have these five needs:

Agree with me the job I should be doing, and the results I
    am expected to achieve
Give me an opportunity to perform
Let me know how I am doing
Give me guidance and training where I need it
Reward me according to my contribution.

In chapter 2 we considered the impact and some of the
potentially key features of the corporate culture. No feedback or appraisal system is adequate without the appropriate attitudes and mentality, the right 'feel' to the
organisation. Appraisal systems have gained a terrible repu-
tation through their malfunction, usually when they were
designed as a substitute for a staff development mentality.

They are part of the answer and need to be integrated into the rest of the answer, but they won't provide a solution by themselves.

It is obvious to say that an appraisal takes place within an existing relationship. A good appraisal will raise that rapport, but the starting point is dependent on trust. The effectiveness and quality of an appraisal depends on the quality of the existing relationship. As such, there must be no major surprises in an appraisal meeting. It can be used to document issues that have already been raised less formally, but trust is easily broken by the emergence of new material, especially negative criticism.

The purpose of an appraisal

Here is a list of thirty-three possible reasons for conducting appraisals. I've found every single one of these reasons overtly declared at some time or other in Christian organisations. They are all potentially valid reasons for having an appraisal scheme too. All of them need doing, but not all of these opportunities are best served by being part of an appraisal process.

1. To say, 'Well done!'
2. Affirming the person.
3. Increase learning.
4. Safeguard the family.
5. To share insights.
6. To enable a decision about moving on.
7. To seek out the correct next placement.
8. To build satisfaction.
9. To discuss problems.
10. To formalise dissatisfaction that has already been aired.
11. To update the senior, to pass information upwards.

12. To promote cohesion, a wider understanding of corporate policy, vision and values.
13. To prevent too much time being spent on fringe work topics.
14. To prevent burnout.
15. To recognise performance.
16. To document performance.
17. To obtain job-holder's feelings.
18. To aid motivation.
19. To assign rewards.
20. To rank.
21. To determine career prospects.
22. To look at both effectiveness and efficiency.
23. To help the relationship with God.
24. To honestly evaluate strengths and weaknesses.
25. To determine and provide the necessary support.
26. To enable people to review their own performance.
27. To provide an opportunity to reflect.
28. To identify and release potential.
29. To help break down staff-management barriers.
30. To provide a safe environment for straight speaking.
31. To rediscover personal vision.
32. To rewrite the job description.
33. To provide accountability, eg to donors.

There is clearly a danger of trying to include too many objectives into an appraisal system and then the system really creaks; there isn't enough time in the meeting to fulfil all these purposes properly. Most appraisals contain four basic components:

To review performance against previously set objectives
To set goals for the future
To identify training needs
To briefly consider possibilities more than twelve months ahead.

You need to identify your own reasons clearly and carefully before launching an appraisal system, but most organisations include these four, and find that these needs are best served within an appraisal. But sort out your reasons for instigating appraisals before the paperwork is devised. Too often, I've seen the assumption that organisations can adopt the paperwork from elsewhere and it will suit them equally well. Not if the paperwork was designed with different purposes in mind.

The practice of appraisal

I would like us to consider ten features about the conduct of a good appraisal.

1. Against what?

The single most important feature of a good appraisal is that performance is measured, not people! Too often, appraisals degenerate into character assassination. When an appraisal scheme is first introduced, there should often be no retrospective component in the first session, if targets are not yet agreed. The measuring criteria must be established before comments on quality or success can be made.

Pitching these criteria at the right level is difficult and is the technical skill that I most frequently find lacking. If the criteria are goals, in SMART form (as in Tool 3), the usual danger is that while they are precise, they are unrepresentative of a year's work. The best thing is to approach the year in terms of KRAs (also in Tool 3), changing each of these features into SMART goal format at interim supervision meetings during the year.

2. Frequency

Usually, appraisals will be conducted annually, but there is a case for a pattern like 3, 9, 21, 33 months, etc. The induction period in a new job is a unique time, and it is useful to set initial goals after three months. Then look at a six-month block with a further formal review after nine months in post. Too often, the first appraisal drifts beyond a full year; bad habits can become established, and it is two years before we really have an opportunity to measure performance against agreed goals. After these two appraisals covering the early months in a post, turn to a more typical twelve-monthly cycle.

3. Advance notification

Give plenty of notice and agree a mutually convenient time.

4. Duration

Allow a minimum of one-and-a-half hours and a maximum of two-and-a-half hours. If it goes on for too long, there is a danger of repetition. More typically, insufficient time is allocated, especially remembering that the early minutes are about settling down and are seldom at maximum efficiency. The appraisee cannot mistake the message of a rushed appraisal: 'You do not care enough about my development.'

5. Preparation

Many organisations have found that a preliminary document has helped to focus the discussion time. It's hard to recover from a bad start to a meeting, so do your homework thoroughly. Have all the paperwork at hand, and do a final check immediately before the meeting commences. Write down the key messages that you want to put over. And above all, pray!

6. The climate

There must be absolutely no interruptions. Seating arrangements should be as though it is a counselling situation, informal and 'equal'.

7. Monitor the process

The appraisal should always be conducted by the immediate supervisor, but there should be access to the 'grandfather' if there is disagreement about the outcome.

8. The timing

Some organisations prefer to do all the appraisals in a compact time span, eg between January and March. Others prefer to spread the additional demands on management time more evenly throughout the year. A decisive factor can be the issue of whether the appraisal is linked to the pay awards. In my experience, about fifty per cent of companies link pay and the appraisal system, usually the companies least interested in the development of their staff. Some organisations deliberately separate the two, eg the pay review is on the first of January and appraisals are conducted between January and March, so that they have the minimum bearing on pay.

9. Maintaining the balance

We must retain a balance on the four dimensions or axes illustrated in figure 24 on page 140. Let's start with the long-term focus and short-term issues. The appraisal offers the opportunity to look a full year ahead, and briefly beyond that horizon, as well as the chance to spot trends in practice and thinking. I find the greater danger is that appraisals are more prone to limit the issues to the short term; goals are set covering less than six months ahead.

Secondly, looking at the overview–detail axis, the more likely problem is that the meeting is hijacked by detail. If you want to make a criticism, start with the generalisation, then give specific examples. But then take the discussion back to the general point, rather than focus on the validity of a par-ticular example for too long. The danger is that the conver-

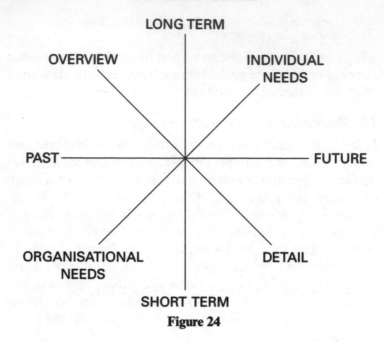

Figure 24

sation ends up with a defence of the particular illustration and misses the bigger issue.

The third balance that must be maintained relates to the past and future. A frequent weakness that I have observed is that too much time is spent discussing the past, with too little emphasis on the future. At least sixty per cent of the appraisal time should be focused on the future; three of the four main purposes listed at the beginning were in the future. Only the review of performance against goals was retrospective.

The remaining dimension is usually held in better balance; there must be development of the individual, but also make sure that the person's contribution still meets the needs of the organisation.

There is in fact a fifth and final balance in the practice of appraisals which does not fit easily on the compass-style diagram above, but it is possibly the most important one.

The appraisee should do more than fifty per cent of the talking!

People are far more likely to do what they articulate than what we tell them.

10. People learn best in different ways

Ideally, they might therefore be best served by different types of appraisal. But in the interests of visible fairness, we usually have to adapt a single system to the needs of a range of people.

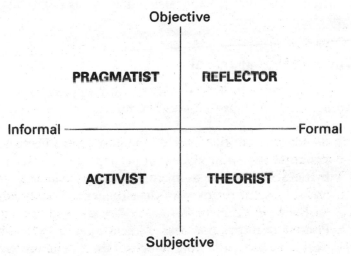

Figure 25. Matching learning styles with types of feedback

The typical annual review suits the reflector admirably. They love it when their superior sits down formally to discuss their work in an objective way. Keep the feedback factual, be as detached and unemotional as possible. The theorist would probably appreciate a longer time allocation than the others. They want all the detail, they have to be convinced to make changes, and they hope for the rationale of your comments. The formal setting is still the more appropriate.

Pragmatists are quite happy to learn without the formality. The rigid appraisal structure may include them so that the system is clearly applied equally to everybody, but their real growth happens in looser situations. They will be content to mix business and pleasure. Activists are least comfortable in a formal appraisal. When you refer back to an incident eleven months ago, they can't even remember the details of last week! Feedback for them has to come very soon after the experience for them to make the mental connections. Reflectors appraising activists is potentially a very fraught situation!

The pitfalls of appraisal

There are many potential reasons for appraisals going wrong. Here are some that I have often seen:

1. Senior staff are not committed to the process. There is an appraisal system in place, but perhaps it was instituted by the personnel department. The most senior staff do not see appraisals or staff development as an integral part of the business.

2. Poor administration, and therefore poor follow-up. There is very little follow-up to the documentation. There is insufficient link between the KRAs and daily activity. Nobody finds the right courses to meet the training needs that we identified, people are too busy to be released or there is insufficient money in the training budget. In time the appraisal system falls into decay because it loses credibility; the system didn't deliver the goods.

3. Wrong corporate culture. The correctly designed system is in place, but there is no overall mentality of staff

development. An appraisal system needs to be an integral part of a policy of the organisation's commitment to people.

4. Low skill levels in the wide number of managers involved in conducting appraisals. Every member of staff with a person reporting to them should be undertaking appraisals.

5. Wrong structures, eg each line manager has too many people reporting to them.

6. Inconsistency over a period of time or across departments. This problem tends to be particularly exposed if the system requires a score (perhaps a range of 1–5) and not just comments.

7. A lack of concern for the subordinate's long-term future.

8. Mistakes made during the interview, eg lack of preparation, either too formal or too informal, hidden agendas, appraisal confused with disciplinary procedures.

9. Wrong attitudes, eg foregone conclusions, bias, negotiating, settling scores, aggression.

10. The paperwork has not been designed to meet the requirements of the appraisal process. It has often been directly copied from another organisation.

All that has been said about the more formal context of an annual appraisal will also apply to the general skill of giving feedback. This will often take the form of encouragement, not criticism. Incidentally, when mixing positive and negative feedback, link them with 'and' not 'but'. There is all the difference in the world between:

'I thought you did really well last Sunday, but did you consider. . . .'

'I thought you did really well last Sunday, and did you consider. . . .'

The principal differences in style between an appraisal and feedback would be that feedback will be shorter, more frequent, more immediate, less formal and less structured. Activists particularly need the feedback to be close to the event; they will forget details very quickly. All that we have said about purpose and practice will remain true.

The concept of 'having a supervision' seems peculiar to social services and allied caring professions. Supervising staff is part of any manager's responsibilities, but in these professions the word usually refers to a formal meeting either monthly or every six weeks, according to the practice of the organisation. In calibre, it is between the immediate, informal feedback preferred by activists and the more significant annual event. It's a great idea and I commend it to all church leaderships. It is the ideal way to unpack the KRAs and put measurable goals under them. The frequency is about right, the context is a little more formal than casual contact, and this ensures that the meeting takes place. It keeps staff development closer to the front of the mind than an annual appraisal.

In finishing this section, I would like to introduce you to Johari's window. No, I haven't gone all Eastern or mystical, the title was coined from the first names of the authors, Joe and Harry!

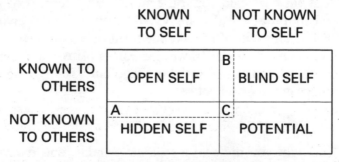

Figure 26. Johari's window

The headings of the rows and columns are self explanatory, but the regions are interesting. Maximising our potential is achieved by increasing the area of the open self. We all have some components within the 'hidden self' region; it's our choice as to when we release those elements. (Bringing region A into the 'open self', by disclosure.) But it needs the help of others to reveal the 'blind self', hopefully with careful timing and sensitivity. (Bringing region B into the 'open self' by having others give us feedback.) Disclosure and feedback offer a fine opportunity to develop people. By a combination of these two methods, region C is drawn into the 'open self' releasing more of our potential.

The key messages from this chapter are:

1. An appraisal system will only be constructive if it is an integral part of a staff development programme and mentality.
2. Different individuals prefer different types of feedback, so use any system flexibly and sensitively.
3. There is nothing wrong with the language of reviewing; it's biblical. But skills and structures are fallible.
4. Don't appraise people, God says that they are worth dying for. Appraise performance against previously agreed criteria.

Action

1. Does your church or organisation have a formal appraisal system? If not, what might the possible benefits be?
2. Good relationships are required for frequent, constructive, informal feedback. Who turns to you for this level of input?
3. How much feedback do you give to the staff members that you directly manage?

4. What parts of your 'hidden self' might be constructively disclosed? To whom? With what possible benefits?
5. The staff that you supervise probably have a 'blind self' region. Are there any areas that you might need to reveal to them? Which areas?

TOOL 8

CHANGING THE MENTAL TAPES

The idea of improving our self-talk is a vital concept in developing leadership, but at times it can be a quite painful and slow process. We are all involved in self-talk virtually every minute, because it includes how we describe and interpret the events around us. Not all of our interpretation is based on sound premises. Albert Ellis analysed these thought patterns and how to improve them. He published his research in 1961 under the general heading of 'rational emotive therapy' (RET). He distinguished between events and emotional reactions to them. The material has a good track record of helping to decrease stress levels, and I felt that this manual needed a practical tool to help leaders in this area, not just an admission that there is plenty of stress around (and within!).

This exercise is designed to uncover particular ideas which contribute to stress. Please complete this questionnaire now; it will probably take about fifteen minutes. Write 'A' if you agree with a statement, and 'DA' if you disagree. It is not necessary to think over any item for too long. Mark your answer quickly and go on to the next statement. Be sure to record how you actually think, not how you feel you ought to think.

1. It is important for me that others approve of me.   ____

2. I hate to fail at anything.   ____

3. People who do wrong deserve what they get.   ____

4. I usually accept what happens philosophically.   ____

5. If a person wants to be, he can be happy under almost any circumstances.   ____

6. I have a fear of some things that often bothers me.   ____

7. I usually put off important decisions.   ____

8. Everyone needs someone he can depend on for help and advice.   ____

9. 'A zebra cannot change his stripes.'   ____

10. I prefer quiet leisure above all things.   ____

11. I like the respect of others, but I don't have to have it.   ____

12. I avoid things I cannot do well.   ____

13. Too many evil persons escape the punishment they deserve.   ____

14. Frustrations don't upset me.   ____

15. People are disturbed not by situations, but by the view they take of them.   ____

16. I feel little anxiety over unexpected dangers or future events.   ____

17. I try to go ahead and get irksome tasks behind me when they come up.   ____

18. I try to consult an authority on important decisions.   ____

19. It is almost impossible to overcome the influences of the past.   ____

20. I like to have a lot of irons in the fire.   ____

21. I want everyone to like me.   ____

22. I don't mind competing in activities in which others are better than I.   ____

23. Those who do wrong deserve to be blamed.   ____

24. Things should be different from the way they are. ____

25. I cause my own moods. ____

26. I often can't get my mind off some concern. ____

27. I avoid facing my problems. ____

28. People need a source of strength outside themselves. ____

29. Just because something once strongly affects your life doesn't mean it need do so in the future. ____

30. I'm most fulfilled when I have lots to do. ____

31. I can like myself even when others don't. ____

32. I like to succeed at something, but I don't feel that I have to. ____

33. Immorality should be strongly punished. ____

34. I often get disturbed over situations I don't like. ____

35. People who are miserable have usually made themselves that way. ____

36. If I can't keep something from happening, I don't worry about it. ____

37. I usually make decisions as promptly as I can. ____

38. There are certain people that I depend on greatly. ____

39. People overvalue the influence of the past. ____

40. I most enjoy throwing myself into a creative project. ____

41. If others dislike me, that's their problem, not mine. ____

42. It is highly important to me to be successful in everything that I do. ____

43. I seldom blame people for their wrong doings. ____

44. I usually accept things the way they are, even if I don't like them. ____

45. A person won't stay angry or blue for long unless he keeps himself that way. ____

46. I can't stand taking chances.   _____
47. Life is too short to spend it doing unpleasant
    tasks.   _____
48. I like to stand on my own two feet.   _____
49. If I had had different experiences I could be
    more like I want to be.   _____
50. I'd like to retire and quit working entirely.   _____
51. I find it hard to go against what others think.   _____
52. I enjoy activities for their own sake, no matter
    how good I am at them.   _____
53. The fear of punishment helps people to be good.   _____
54. If things annoy me, I just ignore them.   _____
55. The more problems a person has, the less happy
    he will be.   _____
56. I am seldom anxious over the future.   _____
57. I seldom put things off.   _____
58. I am the only one who can really understand and
    face my problems.   _____
59. I seldom think of past experiences as affecting
    me now.   _____
60. Too much leisure time is boring.   _____
61. Although I like approval, it's not a real need for
    me.   _____
62. It bothers me when others are better than I am at
    something.   _____
63. Everyone is basically good.   _____
64. I do what I can to get what I want and then don't
    worry about it.   _____
65. Nothing is upsetting in itself – only in the way
    you interpret it.   _____
66. I worry a lot about certain things in the future.   _____
67. It is difficult for me to do unpleasant chores.   _____
68. I dislike for others to make my decisions for me.   _____

69. We are slaves to our personal histories. ____
70. I sometimes wish I could go to a tropical island and just lie on the beach for ever. ____
71. I often worry about how much people approve of me and accept me. ____
72. It upsets me to make mistakes. ____
73. It's unfair that 'the rain falls on both the just and the unjust'. ____
74. I am fairly easygoing about life. ____
75. More people should face up to the unpleasantness of life. ____
76. Sometimes I can't get a fear off my mind. ____
77. A life of ease is seldom very rewarding. ____
78. I find it easy to seek advice. ____
79. Once something strongly affects your life, it always will. ____
80. I love to lie around. ____
81. I have considerable concern with what people are feeling about me. ____
82. I often become quite annoyed over little things. ____
83. I usually give someone who has wronged me a second chance. ____
84. People are happiest when they have challenges and problems to overcome. ____
85. There is never any reason to remain sorrowful for very long. ____
86. I hardly ever think of such things as death or atomic war. ____
87. I dislike responsibility.
88. I dislike having to depend on others. ____
89. People never change basically. ____
90. Most people work too hard and don't get enough rest. ____

91. It is annoying, but not upsetting to be criticised. ____
92. I'm not afraid to do things which I cannot do well. ____
93. No one is evil, even though his deeds may be. ____
94. I seldom become upset over the mistakes of others. ____
95. Man makes his own hell within himself. ____
96. I often find myself planning what I would do in different, dangerous situations. ____
97. If something is necessary, I do it even if it is unpleasant. ____
98. I've learned not to expect someone else to be very concerned about my welfare. ____
99. I don't look upon the past with any regrets. ____
100. I can't really feel content unless I'm relaxed and doing nothing. ____

Complete the score sheet on page 157.

Your scores in the column totals represent your attitude to the following ten irrational beliefs. The lower your score, the less you tend to believe these statements. In his research, Ellis also looked at the frequency of holding these beliefs and they are recorded in order of descending popularity, ie the first irrational belief is the one that is most commonly held. All of these statements have an allied, worthwhile and understandable side, but all of them are destructive in the absolute form outlined below. The irrational beliefs are stated in italics, followed by the explanation.

1. It is an absolute necessity for an adult to have love and approval from peers, family and friends.
Undoubtedly, we all want to be accepted, but even close people who fundamentally like us will not approve of all behaviour and certain qualities. Neither must our actions be driven by the need for that approval.

2. You must be unfailingly competent and almost perfect in all you undertake.

The direct result of holding this belief will be self-blame, since failure is inevitable. As we have already said, perfectionism is the predictable Achilles' heel for those with very high standards. The impossible expectations may be applied to self, others or both.

3. Certain people are evil, wicked and villainous, and should be punished.

It might be fairer to say that certain behaviours are unacceptable or anti-social. The message of grace does not sit comfortably with this irrational belief.

4. It is horrible when things are not the way you would like them to be.

This is the spoiled child mentality at worst. The good side out of the same trait provides a sense of righteous discontent, like a sense of injustice about a situation, but there can be an overwhelming frustration if we apply the attitude to all issues, many of which are outside our immediate control. Things are as they are, not as I want them to be.

5. External events cause most human misery. People simply react as events trigger their emotions.

The logical extension of this false statement is that finding happiness and avoiding sorrow require external events to be within our control. We have choices through our self-talk about how we will react to external events. It is our response to an event that potentially can leave us unhappy, not the event itself.

6. You should feel fear or anxiety about anything that is unknown, uncertain or potentially dangerous.

The fear response must be retained for real danger, then we can enjoy novelty and first-time experiences. I am glad to report personal improvement in this area. Despite reading Matthew 6:25–34, it took a revelation in a stress seminar to produce a breakthrough. Ninety-five per cent of what we worry about is either not worth it, or we can't do anything about it.

7. *It is easier to avoid than face life's difficulties and responsibilities.*
'Never do today what you can put off until tomorrow' is the frequent fruit of this mentality!

8. *You need something other or stronger or greater than yourself to rely on.*
I find many Christians with a high score in this column, who assume that as God is the higher authority, then they are exempt from this fallacy. Actually some of the questions are specifically about the terrestrial sphere. Wise counsel is right, but absolute dependency is not to be envied.

9. *The past has a lot to do with determining the present.*
We do not have to carry all our baggage with us from yesterday into tomorrow. We can learn from the past without being glued to it.

10. *Happiness can be achieved by inaction, passivity and endless leisure.*
Happiness is more than infinite physical relaxation.

Action

The questionnaire is relatively long, but without it the impact of the statements would be very hard to discern. It would be difficult to assess the credibility we give to these irrational beliefs by any direct approach. Go back to the scores and identify the three highest scores, your indicated areas of weakness. Think long and hard about the validity of these scores. You could look back at the cluster of questions which contributed to a particular score, eg if you have a high score in column 5, analyse your answers to questions 5, 15, 25, 35, 45, etc. The actual scores are unimportant; just focus on no more than your top three.

Refuting irrational ideas

Pick a type of situation, based on your scores, that often produces stressful reactions in you.

List the facts, without emotion, judgement or impressions.

Write down your typical self-talk, including predictions, fears, emotions and subjective opinions.

Think about the rational evidence to support the belief or to expose the myth.

What is the worst possible outcome?

What good things might happen?

Change the mental tape and substitute more accurate self-talk.

Because this tool substantially relies on the questionnaire to unearth the nature of our existing beliefs, I have written the whole section as though the reader is going to utilise the material. It's more likely to be a new approach for many readers than some of the other tools.

Remember that the second application is to develop other leaders.

References

The questionnaire is reproduced from *The relaxation and stress reduction workbook*, chapter 10 by kind permission under copyright agreement with New Harbinger Publications, 5674 Shattuck Avenue, Oakland, CA 94609. www.newharbinger.com

Hughes, Selwyn, *A friend in need*, chapter 6 (Kingsway: Eastbourne, 1994).

Dryden, Windy, *An invitation to rational emotive psychology* (Whurr Publishers Ltd.: London, 1994).

Ellis, Albert and Harper, Robert A., *A new guide to rational living* (Wilshire Book Co.: Hollywood, 1975).

BELIEF INVENTORY SCORE SHEET

If your answer *concurs* with the following codes, A or DA, score one point in the box beneath the code. If your answer *differs* from the following codes, score zero.

1.A	2.A	3.A	4.DA	5.DA	6.A	7.A	8.A	9.A	10.A
11.DA	12.A	13.A	14.DA	15.DA	16.DA	17.DA	18.A	19.A	20.DA
21.A	22.DA	23.A	24.A	25.DA	26.A	27.A	28.A	29.DA	30.DA
31.DA	32.DA	33.A	34.A	35.DA	36.DA	37.DA	38.A	39.DA	40.DA
41.DA	42.A	43.DA	44.DA	45.DA	46.A	47.A	48.DA	49.A	50.A
51.A	52.DA	53.A	54.DA	55.A	56.DA	57.DA	58.DA	59.DA	60.DA
61.DA	62.A	63.A	64.DA	65.DA	66.A	67.A	68.DA	69.A	70.A
71.A	72.A	73.A	74.DA	75.A	76.A	77.DA	78.A	79.A	80.A
81.A	82.A	83.DA	84.A	85.DA	86.DA	87.DA	88.DA	89.A	90.A
91.DA	92.DA	93.DA	94.DA	95.DA	96.A	97.DA	98.DA	99.DA	100.A

Column totals

1	2	3	4	5	6	7	8	9	10

IMPROVING COMMUNICATION

All trainers, both good and bad, are ready to deliver courses on communication skills. Among the crowd, I too am frequently asked to put on one-day events on this subject. A few years ago I sensed that I'd lost most of my sparkle on this particular topic. Various delegates who had repeatedly worked with me were kind enough to continue to say nice things, but eventually I gave the problem some serious analysis. I believe that the difficulty was the same problem that many managers and leaders experience: an assumption that there is nothing new to be said on the subject.

Happily, the realisation brought me back with a fresh urgency which motivates me, not only to deliver courses on personal communication skills, but perpetually to strive to improve my quality. The impact of communication on the effectiveness of leaders is colossal. When I was a maths teacher, I often told pupils that time spent on learning their multiplication tables would pay dividends many times over. In exactly the same way

Communication is the core skill and the life-blood of leadership.

Let's review the range of management functions which are in part dependent on these communication skills. Many other skills are underpinned by good communication.

Delegation: As we said in Tool 4, the two key skills are allocating the right job to the right person and communication. At the outset we have to describe the task, the end product in our mind's eye. Monitoring during the process can be construed as constructive or interference. It's the quality of the conversation that determines this interpretation. Similarly, the debrief has the potential to be destructive or a major learning experience.

Selection: The interview is the most commonly used selection tool, and poor interviewing technique is perhaps the most frequent reason for unsatisfactory appointments. Just as in all communications, poor preparation can be a big factor. Remember that the candidate can operate in arousal mode for up to two hours. Subconsciously, they can give you the type of language that they sense is expected. Sharpening interviewing skills is virtually the same as improving communication skills.

Appraisals: The relationship between the two parties starts with their rapport outside the formal meeting. Given the fixed nature of some of the messages during their meeting, communication is the only feature which can enhance or threaten that relationship during the formal component.

Teamwork: We will discuss this thoroughly in Tool 11, but good teamwork involves making decisions together. Various contributions are needed; they are made in very different styles and we don't always hear the gist of different contributions. For a team to be better than the sum of the individual parts requires clear communication and lots of it!

Sharing the vision: The main focus of this book is leadership development, so I won't be tempted very far on the issue of corporate communication. Yet in a way, building and sharing the vision is a key exercise for any organisation. Again, it's based on communication. The second vital ingredient in fulfilling the vision, is the management of change, and once we know where we are going, much of the rest of the challenge is about gaining commitment. The core skill is still communication.

Please then, on this subject of communication skills, where it is difficult to phrase hints in new ways, be realistic about your present skill levels, and remember that even a small improvement will pay vast dividends.

Transmitting

The nature of the difficulty is virtually as old as the hills. Most of us use a very narrow vocabulary, dictionary publishers estimate less than three per cent of the available words. Maybe that's not such a bad thing, since many words have various different meanings (for example, Harper Collins quote eighty-three uses of 'take'). Even Jesus had trouble communicating with his disciples. The Gospels quote three attempts as he tried to tell them about the forthcoming difficulties in Jerusalem (Matthew 16, 17, 20; Mark 8, 9, 10; Luke 9 (twice), 18).

Here are the core ingredients of communication (see figure 27).

Sort out the *aim*, or purpose of the communication, before you start transmitting. Often this might be better phrased as defining what you want the receiver to do, not what you want to say. Oh, that every sermon could start from that premise! Don't always assume that you are the best *communicator* for a particular receiver. Sometimes you have the most familiarity with the content, but not necessarily the best rapport with the receiver.

Usually we focus on three stages:

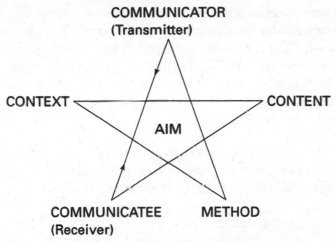

COMMUNICATOR
(Transmitter)

CONTEXT

CONTENT

AIM

COMMUNICATEE
(Receiver)

METHOD

Figure 27. The core ingredients of communication

SPEAKING
HEARING
UNDERSTANDING

The communicator's choice of words might be different if we added:

MOTIVATING
ACTING.

The *communicatee* is the receiver, the person who attributes the meaning. It's not what you said that matters, it's what they decided that they heard. As you reach the end of this book, I know you will believe you understand what you think I said, but I'm not sure you realise that what you heard is not what I meant! The transmitter should be prepared to vary the method and context to suit the receiver.

The *contents* are the ideas that we hope to share, the message. How much detail does this audience require? Is it the first time that the topic has been discussed? What are the preferred learning styles of the receiver(s)? How will you make sure that you have been understood? Do they know you well? The *context* is the setting. A large group or an individual? People who are familiar with technical language about this setting or not? How good are the acoustics of the room? Appropriate *methods* take account of the 'noise' and potential distractions.

Remember that communication is a two-way process. Both parties have responsibilities and both need to take an active role.

As a speaker therefore:

1. Know your aim, including identifying your target audience and your message.
2. Check whether you are the right sender.
3. Keep the message simple.
4. Keep the language appropriate, simple and vivid.
5. Remove the maximum number of distractions.
6. Repeat the message using a different method, until you are certain that the goal has been achieved.
7. Check that there has been understanding.
8. Use face-to-face communication when possible. Consider using writing for confirmation.
9. Use horizontal communication, put the message *across*.
10. Look for and perceive feedback from the receiver and modify your approach accordingly.

There are three elements within a face-to-face communication and researchers have assessed their impact to be:

WORDS	7%
SPEECH	38%
NON-VERBAL	55%

Hence, I am reinforcing the preference for face-to-face communication whenever possible, since only seven per cent of our potential impact can be obtained by writing, and only forty-five per cent down the telephone. Speech includes tone, volume, inflection and speed of speaking. Thus the same words can be interpreted in totally different ways; the options are generated by the tone and the 'filters' that the listener chooses to insert. Incidentally, the ear could be trained to receive up to 500 words per minute although the average adult transmission rate is only 125, not much better than good typing! Don't leave people bored by speaking too slowly; equally, rushing your words, especially when the context is tricky, can be very disconcerting.

I am not going to concentrate substantially on non-verbal communication, except to underline that within transmission it has the most impact. There are two components of non-verbal communication, the 'fixed' and the 'variable'. Choice of clothes, hairstyle, make-up, beards, spectacles, etc, are fixed for any given face-to-face situation; we don't usually go and change a jacket half way through a discussion! The 'variable' revolves around body language, the biggest single contribution to communication. I want you to be aware that high credibility comes when the verbal and non-verbal contributions are congruent and consistent. The non-verbal domain is as ambiguous as the spoken word over a short time span. But when you are the receiver, over a couple of minutes you will have been processing hundreds of messages subconsciously. Trust your gut reaction. It's very easy to illustrate the significance of the non-verbal impact; just watch a play on the television with the volume on zero. Without any words, the themes will still be apparent. You will be quite clear, for example, whether two people are pleased with each other or having an argument. I will never forget visiting the Bolshoi ballet while working in Moscow; without understanding a word, the story-line was easy to follow. Individual words are often relatively unimportant.

Targeting

It's important to think about targeting when you are speaking to groups, audiences or congregations. Who are you especially trying to reach? With how much detail? There should be an observable difference between communication based in regions A and B in the next diagram. Giving the headlines to those who must know, compared with amplifying the communication to include all the detail for those who might want to know, represent opposite ends of the communication spectrum. The more details we choose to include, the greater the risk that some people will miss the headlines. Research indicates that the receiver is not particularly interested in the message for approximately two-thirds of the time. So it is up to the transmitter to give the right amount of detail, making listening as easy as possible.

Headlines	**Region A**		
Some background			
All the fine detail			**Region B**
	Those who MUST know	Those who SHOULD know	Those who COULD know

Figure 28. Communicating at the right level

Listening

Listening is demanding; it requires a very high degree of concentration and is the communication skill that should be most used. Few of us ever received a lesson in listening during our schooling. The emphasis was on writing, the skill we least needed later.

	Listening	Speaking	Reading	Writing
Learned	1st	2nd	3rd	4th
Used	45%	30%	16%	9%
Taught	Least	Next least	Next most	Most

Figure 29. The skills of communication

Whatever the duration of a transmission, generally the meat of the speaker's content is somewhere in the middle, unfortunately during the lowest region of the listener's attention span. So it is vital to identify the headlines at the outset; first impressions are critical because the listener is making a decision about whether to bother concentrating for the rest of the transmission! The importance of the finale is similar. Have you ever heard a sermon, speech or training event and watched the impact on the listeners of phrases like 'And finally . . .' or 'Just in closing . . .' or 'My last point is . . .'. Everybody sits bolt upright. But beware! You can only use one of these tools to focus the mind. False summits are very disconcerting for the listener. I've heard sermons that could have begun with 'And finally' since there was so much content still to come.

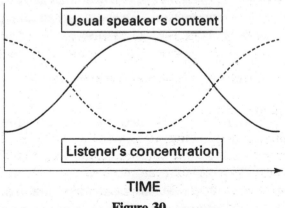

Figure 30

If we want to develop leaders, we will need to work hard on our listening skills. How well we listen will be interpreted as an indicator of how much we care. Future leaders are not our projects, they are individuals with their own agendas, hopes, fears, disappointments and joys. We must gladly minister to the whole person.

Attending

This quaint word is rife in books on communication. Essentially, attending means showing that we are listening. It includes eye contact, nodding (preferably with our eyes open!) and comments like 'Fine', 'Right', 'OK' and 'I see'. But we can be a little more pro-active and use the technique of rephrasing and reflecting. It shows that we are still paying attention and offers the opportunity to correct misinterpretations at the earliest moment. Phrases like these are helpful:

'So if I'm understanding you correctly, you are saying. . . .'
'What you want me to do amounts to. . . .'

The skill is very simple, and this feedback can make a big difference to the transmitter, but it must not be overworked or used to score points. In the two examples above, I wanted the words to sound neutral. We should be equally prepared for an affirming or correcting response.

Questioning

There are various types of question which may be asked for different reasons; I've illustrated some possible groups in the diagram and described some below.

Put-down questions

These aren't really questions at all; they are a device for establishing and maintaining some form of supremacy. They usually contain a negative and are only anticipating one answer.

'Haven't you done that yet?'
'Didn't you finish that last week?'
'You don't expect me to believe that?'

Try to eliminate these from any repertoire. They don't build relationships and they are not effective.

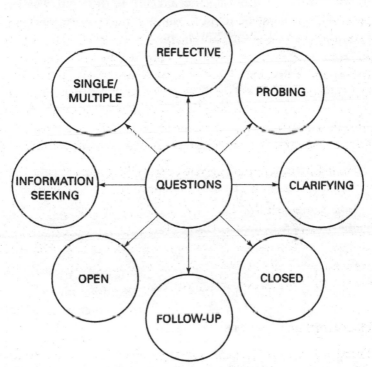

Figure 31. Types of questions

Multiple questions

I think that insecurity and the fear of loneliness have discouraged the acceptability of silence. Instead of being content with a pause, interviewers fill the gap with more questions. Chat shows illustrate the same weakness, largely because they are programmes designed to benefit the host. I've seen it when missionaries return home on furlough:

'Wasn't it dreadful for you to arrive out there without your belongings, and it was in the middle of the rainy season, with the kids changing school as well?'

'Yes.'

'And now you are back here, there is different weather again. There must be lots of other changes since you were home last as well as the church split?'

'Yes.'

Ask one question at a time and allow space for thought and a response.

Closed questions

Closed questions can be answered by a simple 'yes' or 'no' reply.

'Have you done that yet?'
'Did you finish that last week?'
'Do you expect me to believe that?'

They are not good for real exploration or for generating a conversation. But sometimes they are useful to clarify an issue and are much beloved by political commentators.

'Tell me simply, Chancellor, will you be increasing the rate of income tax in your next budget?'

Open questions

As Rudyard Kipling said (*Just So stories*):

I keep six honest serving men
They taught me all I know
Their names are What and Why and When
And How and Where and Who

'When' and 'Where' can still lead to single-word responses; 'How' and 'Why' tend to produce the most significant information.

Single + probe packages

This combination can become very significant as a job interviewing technique. Equal opportunities' policies require that we offer all candidates the same core questions, which may well be closed, but the probes go deeper and enable us to explore further. The gentle introduction also goes some way to putting the recipient at ease.

> 'Have you enjoyed your present job?'
> 'Oh yes.'
> 'What has been particularly exciting?'

Clarifying questions

This type could crop up in a decision-making team meeting. Frequently, we might be asking for a summary to a lengthy contribution, or checking that our own listening was accurate.

> 'Could you just run through the pros and cons again, please. I'm not sure I understand the balance. You are actually in favour of this proposal, aren't you?'

Reflective questions

At first, this structure does not look like a question, but the silence after the statement draws a response. It's a useful technique in all kinds of negotiation, and often produces much better results than a counter proposal.

> 'I suppose that means that we cannot meet on Friday then?'

Information seeking questions

Presuming a neutral inflection, this subdivision is self-explanatory.

'Can you tell me the way to Piccadilly station please?'

'What time shall we meet on Tuesday?'

Sometimes an apparently open question is betrayed by the tone of voice. It is designed to be incisive, with pitfalls for the unwary. This just goes to show that words have very little meaning without taking account of the tone.

As I outlined at the beginning of the section, I wanted to present substantial detail on a relatively straightforward topic. Simply, the impact of a small improvement in communication skills will pay rich dividends. In particular, during the time when the concept of this book was taking shape, and as I have worked as a consultant and informally to develop leaders, the technique of asking questions has yielded many benefits. It is an easy and concrete skill to sharpen. But, much more significantly,

*People are **far** more likely to do what **they** articulate than what **you** tell them.*

A good friend of mine is the equivalent of a bishop in his own denomination. Usually he receives a few phone calls each week from ministers with difficulties asking for advice. He decided that for a month he would give them none, for he realised that too often the advice was tainted by what he personally could and would do, taking too little account of their personalities and competencies. His report to me was that far more problems were solved and the solutions were being sustained.

I've also found that asking questions is the only way you can focus on the medium-term future. Feedback addresses the past, being directive can cover short-term issues, but hopes, dreams and aspirations are not ours to impose. Questions like these have served me well:

'What have been the major successes in the last six months?'

'Anything in particular that you would put them down
   to?'
'Are there any general lessons? Could the same factors
   work for you again?'
'What areas of your work have not gone so well?'
'Have you identified some possible reasons?'
'Which reasons do you think are most likely?'
'Why?'
'What do you hope to be five years from now?'
'What would you like to be doing more of and less of?'
'Which obstacles are the most likely to frustrate you?'
'How would this affect your family?'

Done well, this does not come over as an inquisition!
Within ten questions, over the span of thirty minutes, you
will be addressing real issues, or have received a strong
message that the hearer doesn't want to open up at the
moment. The bigger the issue, the more significant the cross-
roads, the more important it is to ask questions. The key is to
help *them* to think through *their* own solutions to *their* problems.

Action

1. If you are involved in public speaking, have a presentation audio or video taped and analyse it with someone
   you trust. Ask your friend to identify unique features in
   your style, both some good and bad ingredients. Also ask
   them to identify the first moment in the tape where their
   concentration wavers.
2. In the preparation stage of your next public presentation,
   emphasise to yourself more what you want people to do,
   and less of what you want to tell them.
3. Start asking lots more questions!

References

MacKay, Ian, *A Guide to Asking Questions* (Bacie: London, 1980).

Francis, Dave, *Unblocking Organizational Communication* (Gower: Aldershot, 1987).

Back, Ken and Kate, *Assertiveness at Work*, second edition (McGraw-Hill: Maidenhead, 1982).

Adair, John, *Effective Communication* (Pan Books: Great Britain, 1997).

COACHING, MENTORING AND DISCIPLESHIP

Leadership styles

Good leaders know their members and try to vary their leadership styles according to the individual concerned and the situation. Jesus not only undertook the challenge of developing the disciples using personal approaches, he was able to use appropriate styles with Peter at different stages of their walk together. It is not always easy to help leaders acquire and apply additional styles; often they will behave differently with an observer present. What would we be observing? In essence, another way of thinking about styles of leadership would be to call them communication styles. How we lead is largely reflected in our speech.

The main ingredient producing the different styles of leadership is the varying use of authority. There is no definitive answer about when to exercise authority, but three factors should drive the decision which underpins the choice of style:

1. The leader's preferences in style. We are not as flexible as Jesus and operate more comfortably in certain styles than others. Although, using arousal, we can use unaccustomed styles for a short period, we will tend to return to type after a short time span.

2. The maturity and motive profile of the person we are addressing.
3. The context or setting. Our style should be driven by the needs of the situation. If the fire alarm goes, a directive approach is most suitable, not forming little groups to discuss how we are feeling about the situation!

Various authors have made contributions to understanding a range of possible styles. The simplest approach talks of authoritarian, democratic and *laissez-faire* distinctions. While a total of only three styles is too simplistic, a clear recommendation emerged. Generally people prefer to be managed in a consistently involving way. Think back to your school days: the teachers with whom you felt the most secure were consistent about your boundaries; you could get away with the same things every day, and nothing else! It's the consistency that provides the security.

LEADERSHIP STYLES

Authoritarian	Democratic	*Laissez-faire*
By leader	Jointly	By member

RANGE OF USE OF AUTHORITY

Other authors have identified a wider range of approaches. All the styles have a place and are equally valid when applied to appropriate situations. The following table summarises the styles, gives a brief analysis, and an example from the Gospels.

Perhaps surprisingly, I cannot find an example of Jesus using the democratic style with his disciples. It could be argued that the team was never mature enough for him to use the democratic style, although there are many illustrations in the book of Acts and in the epistles.

STYLE	DESCRIPTION	STRENGTHS	WEAKNESSES	EXAMPLE FROM THE GOSPELS
DIRECTIVE	Do it Do it this way	Clear direction Good for control Best option in a crisis	No participation Harsh on failure No initiatives	Matthew 21:1–3 Collecting the donkeys for Palm Sunday
GOAL SETTING	Carrot and stick Objective feedback 'This would be good for you'	High performance Clear authority Challenge	Development still driven by leader High dependency Functional friendships	Luke 10:1–17 The sending out of the Seventy
RELATIONAL	'Do it for me please'	Good harmony High concern No conflict	Low standards Slow decisions Compromises	John 21:1–14 'Simon, do you love me?'
DEMOCRATIC	'Here is the problem. Let's decide together'	Good participation High trust Good ownership of outcomes	Slow decisions Information overload Meetings!	I really cannot find an example between Jesus and the disciples
PIONEERING	Leadership by personal performance	Good example Lots of freedom High attainments	Not supportive No team spirit Leader dependent	John 13:2–17 Washing the disciples' feet
COACHING	On the job training. Skill acquisition	Good encouragement Personal growth Feedback	Low direction Poor in crisis Low corporate communication	Mark 9:17–29 Healing of the boy with a dumb spirit

Figure 32. Leadership styles

Coaching

For the bulk of this section, I want to focus on the last row of the diagram and address the coaching approach, including how it is different from mentoring. Additionally, we will begin to explore how the concept of discipleship interfaces with these tools. The coaching style is an important one for us to explore. I have analysed questionnaire results about leadership styles from over 5,000 Christian delegates at conferences that I have conducted, and the coaching style is the lowest preference. Yet it is the best alternative for power people (see Tool 2) in their development of other power leaders; failure to coach probably means that they will resort to being directive, which is the least developmental and the most likely to produce conflict.

'Coaching' in everyday language is most frequently applied to sport. It involves the transmission of skills from a highly competent person to a pupil. No other authority structure is presumed than the acknowledgement of the coach's technical ability; for example, I have known secretaries coach their bosses in computer skills. The only potential barrier to bridging the skills differential is the boss's dignity! The process of coaching is very time consuming and labour intensive; often it is one to one and seldom takes place outside very small groups. This is the typical model:

The coach demonstrates the skill and the pupil watches.

Repeat the demonstration with the pupil asking questions.

The pupil attempts the skill and the coach gives feedback.

The pupil repeats the skill, improving at most cycles.

The pupil hits a substantial difficulty and the coach demonstrates again.

The pupil incorporates those suggestions.

The pupil goes away, applies the skill in the work context, and only returns if difficulties occur.

The coach monitors the pupil's progress.

This is a slightly narrower definition than the usual sport's coach. Often team 'manager' would better describe what actually happens, and although there are some good managers who were not outstanding players, the best coaches are renowned for technical competence as well as knowledge. For example, in the UK there are two levels of qualification for football coaches; a key difference for the higher award is the ability to demonstrate the skills. When I was playing table tennis at representative standard, Japanese coaches were allowed to work only with players below their own playing ability.

There are many other opportunities for skills transmission. The garage mechanic's apprenticeship was modelled on this pattern as were many other trades; the pay reflected your status before qualifying! Parents can pass on key skills to their children; cooking, sewing, plumbing and electrical dexterity would be examples. Vicars have a similar opportunity to train curates, admittedly the skills are often different! Evangelists can work with trainees in virtually any type of evangelism. Perhaps one of the best settings is in the small mid-week meeting situation, the home-group leader working with an apprentice.

If the first requirement for coaching is an appropriate setting as we have illustrated, the other premise is undoubtedly a very high technical ability in the coach. We need a really accurate assessment of our abilities, a recognition of any 'super skills'. For the potential of coaching to be realised, it is the pupil's affirmation of the skill level that matters, not how we would describe the strengths and weaknesses of our own skills' portfolio. They have to respect the quality and be confident in the relationship. If not, there may be plenty of teaching going on, but not much learning!

A coaching culture

In chapter 2, we talked about the corporate culture. The concepts are of particular importance here so that we produce the right climate to facilitate coaching. I have listed some of the elements below, not that they will be very different from those required for any other approach to good leadership development. These might be the hallmarks of a good climate for coaching:

1. Teamworking and partnerships dominate relationships.
   It is the norm for people to be coached, and the track
   record is that previous pupils are not competitive with
   their enhanced skills. Status issues and individualism are
   frowned upon.
2. Genuine mistakes can be made without a breakdown in
   trust or too much loss of face.
3. Change is on the agenda permanently, both at a personal
   and corporate level. We recognise that change is normal
   and desirable, but the dosage needs managing!
4. We pay more than lip service to the fact that different
   people learn best in different ways.
5. Target setting in daily life is normal. We expect
   measurable criteria to be part of our personal development.

Barriers to coaching

We need to identify the most frequent difficulties. No coaching venture is one hundred per cent successful, and when
things don't go well we might be tempted to conclude that
coaching is wrong rather than strive to improve. Here are
some of the main barriers:

1. By far the most common problem is hostile features in the
   corporate culture. Unfortunately, these are the hardest to
   spot, because we are too close to analyse the culture. The
   barrier with the biggest impact can derail the process of
   coaching right at the outset, before there is any opportunity to see the benefits.
2. The potential student is not as enthusiastic as the coach,
   either because the relationship is not sufficiently secure,
   or the coach's skills are not regarded as adequate by the
   student, or the process was imposed on them.
3. There is no recognition that coaching is a process which
   also has an emotional dimension. A student's history

might include negative experiences which have a dispro-
portionate effect on the learning process.

4. Any training is more likely to be successful if it is
designed to meet an agreed need. The student may not
give the same priority or importance as the coach to the
problem which has been identified.

5. The student does not believe that they have the latent
talent to achieve the coach's goal. In attribution terms,
the cause of failure *will be* internal and fixed. Sometimes
this might actually be true, particularly over a short time
span, but their perception is the decisive factor. The
prospects of success are partly determined by the sources
of the problem and solution, as illustrated in the diagram
below. Success will be more likely when the student identifies the solution.

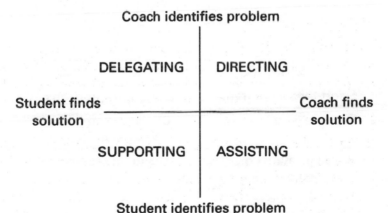

Figure 33. Problems and solutions in coaching

The difference between coaching and mentoring

A mentor takes a longer term view of the process of
development. It is less defined and focuses more on attitudes
and values rather than on skills. Many organisations refer to

the relationship in family language, talking about 'parenting' or the 'elder brother/sister'. The mentor may take responsibility for ensuring that a wide variety of coaches are provided for the student, because different coaches are needed for different skills. The coaching is complete when a certain skill level has been reached. Mentoring will be less formal; there will be a greater interest in the whole person. Technically, mentoring is far more difficult and requires a much deeper commitment. Mentoring is very costly in its demands on time. Yet potentially, the rewards are greater and there is less likelihood of the process being largely for the church's or organisation's benefit; the principal focus is on the person.

The mentor will need all the skills of non-directive counselling, supporting and listening as well as being pro-active. Both student and mentor will jointly need to explore issues of vision, not just goals. The relationship must be more facilitative than directive. In summary:

COACHING	MENTORING
Short-term time frame	Long-term horizons
Focuses on skills	Considers attitudes, values and vision
Based primarily on competence	Based on relationship
Outcomes are more easily measured	Satisfaction and fulfilment are the aim
Addresses technical shortfalls	Ministers to the whole person

Figure 34

Discipling

In the Gospels, Jesus told us to go and make disciples, not merely converts. In practical terms, I find this more demanding expectation is rarely sought in today's churches, for a variety of possible reasons. Part of the explanation is probably that in making disciples we will need to provide both coaching and mentoring. One of the messages from the Gospels is that developing a dozen people in a mentoring way is really an enormous undertaking; coaching is less exacting. Both leaders and members might be reluctant to meet the challenge; either may hope that the need for such commitment can be avoided.

Action

Please think about your answers to these questions:

1. Who have been the most effective coaches and mentors for you?
2. What was it that worked so well for you in your development under their influence?
3. To what extent are coaching and mentoring a recognised part of your organisational culture?
4. When were you last helped to improve in a skill by a peer?
5. Who is still influencing your attitudes and approaches?
6. How do the most senior people in your church or organisation continue to grow?
7. What are your 'super skills' in which you could be a competent coach?
8. Who would accredit you as a coach?
9. Among the people you 'supervise', which of your relationships are so strong that they could potentially lead to mentoring opportunities?

10. What would be the biggest obstacles preventing you from dramatically increasing a coaching or mentoring function? Identify ways of minimising the impact of these obstacles.

References

Megginson, David and Boydell, Tom, *A Manager's Guide to Coaching* (Bacie: London, 1979).

TEAMWORK

Team is a big buzz word; it has a good ring about it, and rightly so. I can honestly say that three of the best experiences in my life have happened in the team context; one of them is my marriage. But two of the most painful times of my life have also been working in a team context; the closer we grow, the greater the potential for friction. Teams are important, they can provide a great opportunity for leadership development, and they may well deliver higher results than the individuals would do working apart. But if we take the biblical pattern, much more seemed to happen through leaders without the aid of a team. So I see teamwork as a vital section in this book, but I'm not advocating that all good things must happen in teams. Many successes are achieved by individuals or autocratic leaders.

Let's start by saying what a team is *not*. It is *not* everybody working under the same roof, however few or many the number of people might be. It is *not* a group of people with the same job description working in different locations. So when the national sales director calls his regional managers together for a meeting, that does not necessarily make them into a team. It depends on what they do when they meet. Finally, a committee is unlikely to be a team; teams are selected but committees are elected. More by chance than design, some committees perform very well.

There are two distinct interpretations of what teamwork means and they have very different implications for us. The first, and too frequent usage, would be that teamwork is primarily about rapport and relationships, virtually in any group context. The application could be to a group of two people or to a company of a thousand employees. Basically improvements in teamworking would be about making changes in the corporate culture.

The second interpretation is much stricter, so now let's formally define a team:

A team is a group of people organised to work together.

From this apparently bland definition come three critical corollaries:

A team has a purpose or purposes

Job descriptions help individuals confine their activity and similarly a team needs boundaries and a mandate. Why does the team exist? What are we here to do? The purposes should be clear before the team is picked; then there will be clear indications of the criteria for team membership. By looking at the agenda and minutes, written or observed, you will get some measure of how the team is spending its time, but there is no guarantee that it is doing what it was originally designed to do.

Most items on an agenda should be there for one of three reasons:

To give out information about. . .
To have a discussion about. . . (hopefully prior to a decision being made)

To make a decision on. . . .

I am proposing that *teams make decisions together*. If none of the agenda items lead to a decision being made together in the meeting, then it's not a team.

A team has a limited membership

The team membership and constituency might change, for example if somebody moves away from the area, but there are still boundaries to the team membership, just as the rules of football impose a limit on the number of players. Similarly, there seems to be an optimum range for teams to make satisfactory decisions together. Most research indicates five to eight people.

Significantly, if you change one member, then you've got a new team. Look at the two diagrammatic versions of a team of five people at work below.

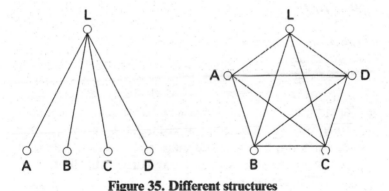

Figure 35. Different structures

Mathematically, I'm going to define A to B and B to A as two relationships. I could treat them as one, it doesn't matter as long as we are consistent. In the first model illustrating leader L and members A to D, if we change one member we change twenty-five per cent of the relationships; replacing

two members would change fifty per cent of the relationships. The structure is quite acceptable; it looks very leader
centred, but it is the best format for a new team or in a crisis
situation.

In the second model, if one member is changed, forty
per cent of the relationships are altered, and if two
members are replaced, seventy per cent of the relationships
are altered. Actually, in a mature team, more like the
second model than the first, the difference is more dramatic than the raw numbers indicate. If one member, eg
B, is replaced, not only are all the relationships involving B altered, but in practice it becomes a new team. By
removing B's contributions, values and expectations, *all*
the other relationships change as well. If you're not
delighted by maths, please trust mine! Just remember the
conclusion:

*If you change one member, you've got a new
team.*

A team has a context or setting

Poor teams try to operate as though they are in a vacuum,
good teams are aware of what is happening around them. If
the purposes and the personnel stay the same, the challenges still vary. Suppose the members of a Baptist church
diaconate were transported from rural Suffolk to inner
London. The team would be the same people doing similar
business, but London is different from Suffolk. Another
parallel, and more realistic, would be to keep the same
people as leaders in the same church for a long time
without them thinking about the changing social, spiritual
and economic climate. Leading the church in 2005 will be
different from today, even for the same group of people.
I've seen too many teams metaphorically trying to invent a

wheel because nobody was aware of the outside world. We need to understand our geographical and chronological context.

Process

Good teamwork is about understanding the value of different contributions and knowing how they can be integrated. In sports parlance, you might have the right players on the pitch, but you also need to use them appropriately. You don't send your goalkeeper to take the corner kicks. It is about timing, encouraging and integrating the appropriate contributions. Please don't underestimate the significance of this. I've met some potentially excellent teams that fall well short of fulfilling their capability because there is no structure to the decision-making process. It ends up as a free for all. Teamwork means that we require different contributions, but that doesn't mean that we find all of them comfortable, or even fully understand the significance and validity. We need the right contributions and a strict adherence to process.

Quite the most powerful research on teamwork was conducted by Dr Meredith Belbin, and published nearly twenty years ago. He said that whatever the task of the team, there are common types of contribution that are needed for all decisions (see figure 36 on page 188).

Most people can contribute two of these functions naturally. One reason for recommending that there should be five to eight people in a team is so that all the roles can be covered. But Belbin talked very little about the process of integrating these contributions and a model like the one in the following diagram brings a vital addition to his insights. It can be followed for every decision, no matter how complex or trivial. The stages are in the boxes across the centre of the diagram (see figure 37 on page 189).

TITLE OF STYLE	FUNCTION	POSITIVE CHARACTERISTICS	PERMISSIBLE WEAKNESSES
Plant	Source of original ideas	Creative, unorthodox, imaginative	Impractical, unrealistic
Monitor evaluator	Accurate judgement	Pragmatic, detached, clear thinking	Cold, clinical, critical, uninspiring
Resource investigator	Knows the team's context, brings fresh information	Wide outside contacts, extrovert, inquisitive	Does not sustain interest, little task focus
Completer finisher	Finishes the job Dots 'i's and crosses 't's	Attention to detail, thorough, precise	Low people skills, perfectionist nit-picking in details
Company worker	Strategic planning	Practical. diligent Administrative skills Structured thinker	Inflexible, conservative
Teamworker	Oils the wheels Listens and interprets Brings harmony	Relational, sensitive, accepting	Avoids confrontation Indecisive Low emphasis on results
Chairperson	Integrates the individual contributions Holds the process to the agenda	Accepting of diverse contributions Clear sense of purpose and direction	Not necessarily creative or academic
Shaper	Challenges the mediocre and the slow Strives for the best	Dynamic, lots of drive, passionate	Tetchy, irritable, intolerant

Figure 36. Team roles

A MODEL FOR TEAM DECISION MAKING

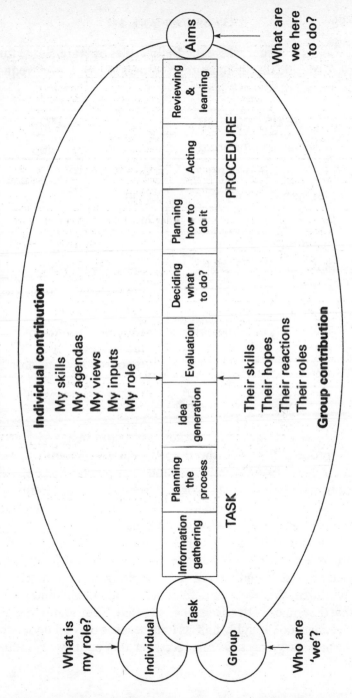

Figure 37

Let us consider where the Belbin roles operate. Some function specifically at one stage, others make more frequent contributions.

STAGE OF PROCESS	CONTRIBUTOR
Information gathering	Resource investigator
Planning the process	Chairperson
Idea generation	Plant
Evaluation	Monitor evaluator
Deciding what to do	The whole team
Planning how to do it	Company worker
Acting	One, or some, or all, or delegated
Reviewing and learning	Many but seldom plant, teamworker or resource investigator

Figure 38

The shaper and teamworker could chip in at any stage of the process. Typically, the shaper might say, 'Come on, we've been here twenty minutes and got nothing done yet!' Contrastingly, the teamworker's role might be, 'John, I am not sure you quite understood what Fred was saying there; just give us the gist of that again Fred.'

One company that I worked with adopted this model for every decision made by the senior management team. It is a medium-sized building firm. Their meetings became much more structured, they enjoyed them more as individuals, and are sure that they made better decisions as a result. They found that team meetings took roughly half as long because they all understood the necessary stages. During recession, they continued gradually to expand the business and the managing director attributed the success to the improvements made to the senior team meetings.

The stages of team development

We now need to look at how teams develop since they go through recognisable, if not distinct phases. John Adair is often credited with the bulk of these insights but four other authors, Matthew, Mark, Luke and John were saying similar things centuries earlier! Good teams are supposed to maintain a creative tension between the needs of individuals, task needs and team dynamics. This balance isn't easy; most tensions that I know are not creative at all!

We do not build the team by giving equal attention to all the elements throughout the life of the team. Recognition of which element should take precedence is critical to the process of team building. The answer lies in this sequence.

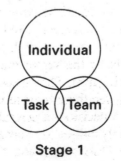

Stage 1

It might sound an apparent contradiction, but in the earliest stages of building a team, the emphasis is on the leader, not the other members. The leader recruits and selects, and the leader sets the corporate culture and models the values. It's not the first decisions that matter, it's how they are made. If the bulk of the contributions are made by relatively few people, then a pattern will be established. If meetings start late, that becomes acceptable practice. If one person is the butt of the first few jokes, then again patterns are set.

A difference of values leading to a desire for different cultures needs open recognition and serious discussion. This is one possible reason for a sort of honeymoon period within a team. It takes time for people to realise that difficulties are now arising in making most decisions rather than only a few. If that is what is happening in your teams, then it's probably a value issue at the root, and it won't go away lightly.

In the Gospels, this initial phase is documented in the first nine chapters of Luke, up to the sending out of the seventy disciples. The focus was strongly on Jesus; the disciples watched and learnt. They began to understand his way of doing things. Clearly also, the disciples were committed to him personally (John 2:11) not to the project or each other.

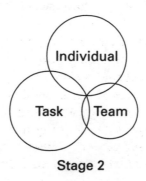

Stage 2

In the second phase, results become much more important. Part of my definition of a team is that it has a purpose, a reason for existing. Teams need to know their function and do well against stated criteria. We aim for effectiveness and efficiency: to be effective we need to know these purposes. But if the *modus operandi* is also clearly understood by the team members, the work will progress smoothly. If there is a sudden change in the personnel of the team, the leader may consciously have to revisit stage 1: 'This is the way we do things here.' For example, the purpose of the leadership team in a church might be:

To oversee the pastoral care of the whole flock
To give vision and direction to the church
To be both a support and a sounding board for the leader.

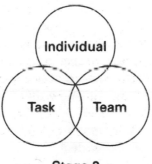

Stage 3

In the final phase, there needs to be a growing emphasis on the personal dynamics and potential synergy within the team, with the target that we are more productive working together than the sum of the individual constituent parts. Some people who would regard themselves as 'teamly' try to rush to this stage without going through the other two. It's a predictable recipe for conflict if the values are not identified and articulated. Only in John 14–16 did Jesus really focus on the team, at the Last Supper, right at the end of his time with them. Even then, their oneness was largely in himself as the leader, and with a clear understanding of the task. Probably the other danger is that leaders with too great an emphasis on the task don't bother to try to reach stage 3. Building a team takes time; it's just whether you see it as a waste of time or as an investment. Generally the returns on the investment are actually greater productivity, as well as higher morale, a lower turnover of membership and less conflict.

The importance of teamwork in developing leadership

1. In Tool 2, we discussed motive drives and discovered that statistically nearly a quarter of the population are high in affiliation motivation only. They will produce excellent results working in teams, but their satisfaction is not based on the results, it's about being with people. There is no excitement in being asked to make the coffee after the church meeting by themselves, but a rota in pairs is fine. Researchers used to think that the affiliation motive led people to waste time, but now there is wide acceptance that it is a legitimate drive. In developing leaders who are strong in affiliation motivation, and there aren't many of them, the team setting is ideal.

2. Inviting potential leaders to a team meeting is a very useful training opportunity, especially if the meetings are good! You don't have to give them a vote or permanently elevate them; it can be made clear that their role is largely observation. We would be exposing them to strategic thinking, overview language and discussion of long-term issues. We can enhance their ability to think along these lines. Progressively, we might ask for a few comments from the trainee leader, giving us an ideal forum to assess them further.

3. Any opportunity for us to exhibit teamwork will be an important learning experience for the trainee; what we do will speak much louder than lecturing. We can model good teamwork to them.
4. The team is where many leaders with ultimate seniority find their accountability. I believe passionately in teams, I believe in an ultimate leader, and I believe in leaders who are truly accountable within their teams. Again, it is good for budding leaders to see accountability being practised.

Action

1. Make a list of the team members that you are developing. Which of them might learn most from a team setting? Which members find it hard to learn from a mentor or coaching environment but listen attentively to their peers? Consider for each, the things that they might learn from a team situation.
2. Are there any members who might learn by attending the senior leadership team meetings regularly, but in a non-voting capacity? Would the rest of the team be comfortable with any of these extra people? Obviously, only consider members who might realistically be part of this team at some stage in the future.
3. What elements of coaching and mentoring might be best achieved in a group setting? For which people?

References

Cormack, David, *Team Spirit* (Marc Europe: London, 1987).

Craig, Sue, *Make Your Mark* (McGraw-Hill: London, 1997).

Bruce, Alexander Balmain, *The Training of the Twelve*,

fourth edition (Keats Publishing Inc.: New Canaan, Connecticut, 1979).

Belbin, R. Meredith, *Management Teams* (Heinemann Professional Publishing: Oxford, 1981).

Hastings, Bixby and Chaudry-Lawton, *Superteams* (HarperCollins: London, 1986).

CONCLUSION

One of the organisations where I deliver training courses has instituted a new practice across their training programme. Previously delegates were sent a certificate of attendance, proving that they had been to the course. At the end of courses now, delegates are required to fill in a form called 'Learning into practice'. It involves setting goals as a result of the new information and skills that have been gleaned from the course. I wholeheartedly applaud this system. Certainly in the training field, I am sceptical of too much knowledge that does not lead to practical benefits. In a similar way, my satisfaction from this book can only come from the knowledge that the content has been beneficial to the readers, on a practical and sustained basis.

I want to make the application, therefore, as easy as possible. What might be your barriers to implementation? How easy or hard is it to apply some of the tools that I have outlined? Let's look at some handy tips to facilitate change in our own lives.

1. Do something. Don't try and do everything!

My experience in training work indicates that the sooner you set a few 'Smart' goals from your learning, the better.

If you put this book back on the shelf, mentally noting that it might be a good idea to pray about the possibility of considering action at some unspecified date in the future . . . then I'm sure that nothing will happen. You need to have committed yourself to action within a week of finishing reading. Between three and seven goals would be ideal.

2. Personal vision is vital

There is a great deal of confusion surrounding words like purpose, vision and mission and some apprehension of the concepts that the words represent. While it would be fun to help you sort these issues out at an organisational level, this book has focused on personal growth and development, so I will resist the temptation. But personal vision is the framework where growth can take place.

Vision essentially answers these questions:

What do you want to become that you are not already?
What do you expect to be thanking God for in x years time in your life?

Vision is *not* about answering:

What will I have done?

What we will have done are the cairns on the way to the summit, not the destination itself. There is no yardstick for distinguishing a good plan from a bad plan without knowing the destination.

Plans are seldom exciting unless there is a mental image of the destination. For the Israelites, stomping around the desert for forty years was the outcome; it wasn't even the plan. It was the promise of 'a land flowing with milk and honey' that kept them going, just! As I hinted briefly earlier in the book, questions about vision are very legitimate questions. God wants us to have personal hopes.

'May he give you the desire of your heart and make all
    your plans succeed' (Psalm 20:4).
'Delight yourself in the Lord and he will give you the
    desires of your heart' (Psalm 37:4).

Clear personal vision is imperative for both changing and learning. Put at the most simple level, if we are not going anywhere, we don't need any tools to get there. How can the tools of this book help you fulfil your personal vision?

3. Discontent

To some people, discontent will be a strange word to focus on at the conclusion of an optimistic book. Contentment has a nice ring to it, but actually it is only a couple of steps from complacent and apathetic on the scale that I have illustrated in figure 38 on page 200. An increase in the level of discontent is constructive, up to a certain point. Beyond the peak of the graph, the discontent hurts more, and provides less prospects of moving forward. There is also a difference between discontent and malcontent, and the distinction is in the motivation, the origins. Malcontents always believe that the grass is greener on the other side. Their attitude is not constructive.

Discontent provides the impetus for improvement. If you are not happy with the market share of your company, with the social injustices that still need to be addressed, with the low numbers attending your church, then hopefully a drive is generated that moves you to action. The book of Haggai is sharpened by the prophet's discontent and Habbakkuk starts off with a four-verse complaint to God about the state of the nations. Applying the principles to our own lives, there needs to be some recognised shortfall, an area where we are very conscious that progress still has to be made. If these concerns are within the leadership field, then there is a prospect that this book can help you.

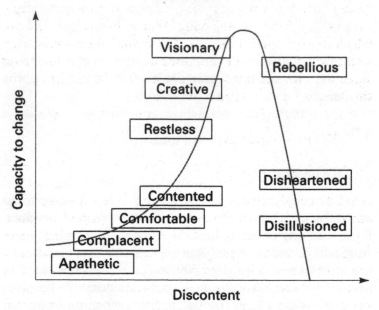

Figure 38. Harnessing discontent

4. The knowledge of the first steps

The long-term vision is necessary to initiate change, but not sufficient. There are a few dreamers with vision who seem unable to commit themselves to action. Sometimes the cause is because of the incomplete nature of the picture. They want all the details of the plan before commencing the journey. Emotionally the small details may feel important, but in practice they can be a cause of difficulty. Unforeseen circumstances require flexible planning. All you need is the vision and the first steps. I gained a great deal from doing a Bible study on the word 'first', but my concordance offers very little encouragement to research 'second' or 'third'!

I found a similar analogy when I was fell walking in the Lake District. If you know the peak that you are attempting, the next key is the starting point. Where do you leave the car, which stile do you clamber over? After that, the route is often well cairned, and small variations in your chosen path over short stretches are not significant. In the bigger picture, the theme is ever onward and upward.

5. Celebrate significant landmarks

My wife and I enjoy gardening. Sometimes when we have completed a section, I will say, 'Right, what shall we do next?' The reply usually involves a cup of tea, a slower pace and the opportunity to take stock of the 'finished' product. I know that finished is a relative term in gardening; there will more weeding, fresh planting next year and basically the job is never done. Developing leadership has a lot of parallels; there is always something else that can be done and the task is never finished. I believe that this makes it even more important to celebrate significant landmarks. Enjoying these celebrations to the full minimises the dangers of the treadmill mentality. The opportunity might be the launch of a training programme, the team jointly identifying their Key Result Areas for the year, or surpassing last year's targets. I think that the same balance is important in our prayer life; we need both thanksgiving and petition.

6. The price of change

Real quality doesn't come on the cheap. We looked in Tool 1 at the temptation of trying to take short cuts. Mentoring and discipleship are expensive processes to all the parties involved. Personal changes have an emotional price and there will be seasons in the process when emotional reservoirs are low and therefore progress will be minimal. Frustration can set in, to either party. The second major cost will be time. Many of the people we hope to develop will be in their thirties, still rightly on the promotional ladder at work and bringing up a family that will only be young once. Even the additional demand of perhaps one extra evening per fortnight, on a sustained basis, is substantial.

7. Additional reading

I know full well that every section in this book could usefully be twice as long. Originally, I was going to write the whole book on the subject of delegation, as a tool for development. If your learning styles are predominantly reflector or theorist, you might like to do some extra reading around a preferred tool. I also know that the second read or exposure to some of these subjects is often when the enthusiasm is really caught.

My desire is that you are convinced of the importance of developing yourself and the leadership team around you. Remember that you have that responsibility for those who are accountable to you. Hopefully, you have been able to use this book as a manual and you will probably have developed the use of the different tools to different degrees. It's important now to review the tools:

Which tools have you learnt most from yourself?
Which tools have you most enjoyed using with others?
Which tools have been most effective with others?

A few years ago, I was involved in delivering a series of one-week seminars throughout the old Eastern bloc. The host was a major international relief agency and their regional co-ordinator introduced all the events. His usual text was 'And the things you have heard me say in the presence of many witnesses entrust to reliable men who will also be qualified to teach others' (2 Timothy 2:2). If the experience has been good to you and for you, please share the principles with others.

If you would like training or consultancy in the principles and skills covered in this book, you can contact:

Bryn Hughes
3 Pound Bank Close
West Kingsdown
Sevenoaks
Kent TN15 6UA
Tel/fax: 01474 854774

Liberated to Lead

by Colin Buckland

This unique book is designed to enhance the effectiveness of full-time leaders in Christian ministry or mission. Used prayerfully, the exercises and points for reflection will enable you to:

- balance family life and the pressures of ministry

- cultivate a healthy attitude to power in ministry roles

- settle on realistic expectations in ministry

- gain an introduction to self-awareness skills

- clarify your sense of calling to Christian service

- avoid unnecessary sexual problems

- overcome or prevent burnout

REVD COLIN BUCKLAND has more than 23 years' experience as a pastor, and more than 18 years' as a consultant, trainer and counsellor to church leaders, churches and Christian organisations.

*FUTURE***CHURCH**